SHILOH

John B. Stephenson

SHILOH:
A Mountain Community

UNIVERSITY OF KENTUCKY PRESS
LEXINGTON: 1968

PRINTED IN THE U.S.A.
LIBRARY OF CONGRESS
CATALOG CARD NO.
68-55044

To Jane Ellen

&

my parents

Preface

This study has its origin in my interest in mountain people and the changing society in which they live. That there are problems in the mountain region calling for understanding is testified to by the recent organization of regional, state, and federal agencies charged with the specific mission of combating such problems. Appalachia in general, and the Southern Appalachian Region specifically, has been recognized officially as a multiproblem area. Depressing statistics on unemployment, dependency, low income, lack of education, infant mortality, and other indicators of social malaise abound. But before these statistics can take on full meaning, I think we must understand what they reflect in the local societies within the region. What is the nature of the local social order? How is it changing from what it was in the last generation? How are the mountain people affected by these changes? Are the regional statistics an outgrowth of the inability of old social structures and old personal adaptive styles to cope with the new order? I hope that the study reported here will help in some way to answer these questions.

My interest in the mountains has not always been so problem-centered. In fact, I, like many people raised in and near the Appalachians, was not so aware that we had such problems until someone informed me. I had always thought of the mountains as a fine place to visit and an even better place to take up residence, except that I couldn't afford to live there. Only later did I realize that I wasn't the only person who could not afford to live there —many of the people living there couldn't afford it either.

But they were sticking it out anyway, taking it rather than leaving it, in Rupert Vance's words. Only gradually did I come to realize that the people referred to by Michael Harrington—and Harry Caudill and John F. Kennedy and Vance and the *Saturday Evening Post*—were the same ones I had as neighbors and school friends when I was a child. In truth, I still think of the mountains as a corner of heaven first and a national disgrace second. And I think of the mountain people as good, kind, rough, gentle friends before I think of them as poverty cases, social problems, or flies on the nation's face.

My chance to combine this longstanding feeling of closeness to the mountains with concern for the problems of the people came in 1965 at the University of North Carolina. Beginning in 1954, some members of the Social Research Section of the Division of Health Affairs and the Institute for Research in Social Science of the University of North Carolina undertook a case study of community social processes and their health relevance in a mountain community, which I shall call Shiloh. Under the direction of Harvey L. Smith, this study has been divided roughly into three stages. The first phase, involving a delineation of stresses operating in the community in the wake of recent rapid social change, has been reported by Smith and by Berton H. Kaplan.[1] The second phase, modified somewhat and presented in this book, is a study of the adaptive patterns of different types of families which have responded differently to the stresses described in previous studies.[2] The proposed third phase

[1] Harvey L. Smith, "Society and Health in a Mountain Community," working paper of the Social Research Section of the Division of Health Affairs and the Institute for Research in Social Science, University of North Carolina, Chapel Hill, 1963; Berton H. Kaplan, "Social Change, Adaptive Problems, and Health in a Mountain Community" (unpublished Ph.D. dissertation, University of North Carolina, 1962).

[2] John B. Stephenson, "Patterns of Adaptation in a Changing Mountain Community: Stress and Health" (unpublished Ph.D. dissertation, University of North Carolina, 1966).

"will involve the closer study of individual members of the same family who appear to have adapted quite differently when confronted with the same stressor."[3] Earlier fieldwork, in 1954, involved a preliminary description of the community setting by Reuben Reina, later analyzed and reported by Ida Harper Simpson.

Another interest gained increasing importance as the study progressed: the processes of change and modernization and their effects on community and family life. Considerable space here is given to describing and contrasting traditional and modern ways of life before the subject of adaptation is introduced. The reason for this arrangement is that the personal and sociological significance of stress and adaptation is tied not only to the present structure of the community but also to the past out of which this present is emerging. I believe that a study such as the present one can contribute a useful set of data to the gradually accumulating number of case studies of modernization carried out by sociologists and anthropologists, making fruitful comparative study of modernization processes and consequences possible.

The final products of the research are, then, a descriptive case study of a number of families living in a changing Appalachian community, a typology constructed on the basis of what is learned about their characteristics, their problems, and their modes of adaptation, a description of the consequences for a mountain community of contact with the mainstream of modern American society, and some observations about successful and unsuccessful adaptation among different family types.

The community described here, unlike most Appalachian communities that have been studied, is one in which the impression is that of overall success in working out adaptive problems. The study draws attention to the frequently neglected "middle-class" mountaineer, pointing

[3] Smith, "Society and Health," 9.

out that he has problems of his own, different from those of the low-income mountain man. The research especially draws attention to the "transitional" mountaineers and the problems they face in living between two cultures.

It is my hope that this study will increase our understanding of Appalachia and, more generally, of the nature of modernization processes, of the effects of social change on families, of the modes of adaptive response to change-induced crises, and of the differences between the families that ride the wave of change and those that are crushed under it.

The questions people have asked me about the study indicate that there is an interest in the methods used as well as in the findings, and to answer some of these questions I have included a methodological appendix to this study. A number of people have asked what I think is required for acceptance into such a community as Shiloh. This problem is particularly challenging for a researcher among Appalachian people, who have a reputation for strong independence and taciturnity. I personally doubt that there is any great secret, because the mystique of the people has been largely exaggerated. The reputation is a caricature and therefore partially inaccurate. Little, if any, threat to safety exists for the outsider; violence is usually reserved for lifetime acquaintances. The taciturnity and independence are simply the natural reserve of a people who prefer to wait until the outsider proves himself before they allow him a deeper knowledge of themselves. Thus here, as with the most meaningful human relationships anywhere, what is required is that one demonstrate trust, warmth, openness, and an ability to contain intimate knowledge. Perhaps the rest of us take our social relationships too lightly. At any rate, though it seems true to me that not just anyone can carry out fieldwork in Appalachian communities like Shiloh, success will depend not so much on extrinsic qualities like speech and appearance as on such less definable qualities as human kindness and courtesy, patience, sympathy, humility, courage, a sense of fairness, a sense of humor, and an interest in understanding the people from their own points of view. These are the same qualities one looks for in any man.

My earliest intellectual debt is to my high school teachers, among them Charles Gartlan, who predicted this book. My interest in sociology and my initial orientations to it are the products of skilled artists at the College of William and Mary in Virginia, chief among them R. Wayne Kernodle and Edwin H. Rhyne. It was also Wayne Kernodle's droll "painter tales" and ramp stories which, together with my own origins in the Valley of Virginia, gave rise to an early personal and academic interest in the Appalachian Region.

To the influence of these men I must add that of Rupert Vance, Gerhard Lenski, and especially Harvey Smith and the entire Miller Hall group at the University of North Carolina. Without their support, encouragement, and helpful criticism this work would have remained the faint glow of an idea.

Contents

I. *Shiloh: Then and Now*

Shiloh is an area covering two or three square miles, little of which is densely populated. It is a series of neighborhoods or localized dwelling areas, together with a few isolated individual dwellings, considered by local people as a geographic and social entity to be distinguished from other such areas nearby. It is more a neighborhood cluster than a community as that term is used in common parlance. There is usually more significant interaction within neighborhoods than between them, and some of the neighborhoods are socially ranked residential areas.

The neighborhoods are linked not only through social identification but also by dependence on some of the same basic services. There is one grade school which serves all these neighborhoods and some beyond. All older children from this section of the county attend the same high school. Not all neighborhoods have their own stores; two stores on the main road carry most of the local trade. Churches are scattered through most of the neighborhoods, but draw their congregations from the whole set of neighborhoods and not just the ones in which they happen to be located (though there is a tendency for residence area to be associated with choice of church attended). The structure of work is also something that tends to knit neighborhoods together, since many men and women from different neighborhoods commute to work together, while others work together in local mining operations, lumbering, farm work, and the like. "Galacking" groups, however, tend to be family groups or neighborhood groups.[1] Finally, the neighborhoods are cemented together to a degree by family ties. Related families tend to live in the same neighborhood, but it is also unusual to find a family that has no kin—at least a second cousin or an uncle by marriage—in the other neighborhoods.

It cannot be said that these neighborhoods are especially internally close-knit, though they are somewhat more cohesive than the community that they make up. Nor are these areas always easily identified. Their boundaries are fluid, and individuals have important reference groups outside their neighborhoods. Some people do not live in anything that could realistically be called a neighborhood. Nevertheless, the neighborhood concept appears to be important for a general description of the ecological nature of Shiloh. Most of the approximately 250 households in Shiloh could be said to belong in one of the twelve to fifteen neighborhoods.

The ecology of the community itself has changed since 1940. For one thing, the neighborhoods within it are not as self-contained as they once were.[2] As one man put it, "There used to be a lot of little communities around—where you would find a little store, a little church, a little school, and a little post office." Another said:

> What used to be called Shiloh was just that part around Silver Creek. This section down here was called Yale. It had a post office and the old Yale school. It used to be that you could go up a little cove and find a few houses, a store, a post office, and a little school and a church, and that would be called a community. But not any more. The schools are

[1] Galax is a small plant with large, hardy green leaves used in the florist industry and purchased locally by evergreen wholesalers at between one and two dollars per thousand leaves. The picking of galax and other evergreens, such as Lycopodium, is usually carried out in family and neighborhood groups and is an important source of income for many economically marginal families.

[2] See Everett M. Rogers, *Social Change in Rural Society* (New York: Appleton-Century-Crofts, 1960), 133-35, and Roland L. Warren, *The Community in America* (Chicago: Rand McNally, 1963), 22-25, for discussions of the decline of the neighborhood in rural America.

> consolidated, the small post offices have been closed down, people go longer distances to bigger stores. So Shiloh extends further than it used to back in those days.

The consolidation of postal services had taken place seven years earlier; the Shiloh post office had been eliminated in favor of rural delivery. "Now, everything is just Route 2, Centerville [the county seat]," as one lady said.

Neighborhood stores are squeezed out as local residents travel farther to get supermarket variety and prices; one store went out of business during the study period. Radio commercials advertise the advantages of driving to town to save money, and a storekeeper complains that television has influenced customers to expect wide selections and the latest products on his shelves.

Thus, the area known as Yellowjacket used to be considered separate from Shiloh, as did the area once known as Frog Branch. Both these places had their own post offices; now the mail is delivered. With two exceptions, the little stores that remain are marginal enterprises at best. ("I keep track of my accounts by using the bills that come in," said a lady storekeeper. "That way, you don't have to make a record of your daily sales—if you have any.") The neighborhood schools have been closed down. The three separate neighborhoods have gradually merged.

Such factors as improved roads and telephone installation have played a part in this merger of neighborhoods, in addition to the processes of consolidation and removal of services from small areas. Indeed, changes in transportation and mass communication must be counted as one of the two most important general areas of change in Shiloh, the other being changes in the economic and work structures.

In addition to the breakdown and merging of neighborhoods, another ecological process at work in Shiloh has involved the gradual movement of the population toward main roads. No actual count was made of new houses with regard to their location because the pattern was clear from the first casual observation: the newer looking the house, the more the likelihood of its being near the highway. It also seemed that the closer a person lived to the main road, the higher his local social ranking and the more acculturated he was in terms of "outside," middle-class society.[3] This ecological change indicates that the population of Shiloh is gradually moving toward the outside world.

Changes in transportation, mass communication, and education are considered together here because their net effects have been the same: the lowering of barriers between Shiloh and the rest of the world. It would not be accurate to say that Shiloh was completely isolated before World War II, but it is clear that the little valley in which it is located has opened up significantly since the war. New roads have been laid, and old roads have been paved. A major mountain parkway and other new and improved highways nearby, as well as connecting roads between them, have allowed a much greater inflow and outflow of traffic than was possible before. Tourists and summer residents come into the valley in greater numbers each year, bringing in outside money and ideas. Fifteen new summer or retirement residences have been purchased or built by persons from outside the area in the five-year period from 1961 to 1965, bringing the estimated total to thirty-seven.

Local residents who in the past walked, rode mules, or hitched rides with more opulent neighbors now own cars or trucks. The number of vehicles reported for tax

[3] For a similar finding in a Dutch village, see B. Benvenuti, *Farming in Cultural Change* (Assen: Van Gorcum, 1962), 376-82.

purposes in the township grew from 80 vehicles in 1949 to 160 vehicles in 1957 and to 437 in 1965.

Craig Bowman, a storekeeper, recalls: "The thing that stands out in my mind about [1946] is that there were no cars then. Dad bought an old truck when he went into the store business, and I can remember he made deliveries in that truck all over this section. . . . Now everybody drives to the store. I can remember people on Silver Creek getting their licenses to drive when they were in their thirties and older. And now everybody has a car."

In a later conversation, Craig also revealed that trade with summer people and retired couples was helping his business, and he acknowledged that the transient tourist traffic was on the increase:

> I asked Craig if tourists had had much influence on his business at the store. He claimed that they had had an appreciable increase in trade with summer residents and retired people, but little from the type of tourist who is just passing through. He said he had seen more cars from Florida passing through this summer than he ever had before. I told him he had better prepare to see an increase in this type. In the next half-hour, five cars from Florida pulled up as if on signal. In that same length of time only three local people came in to trade. Although that half-hour was not representative, it was enough to make Craig think again.

Better roads and more cars have also made possible such new patterns as commuting to work, frequent changes of residence, school consolidation, more frequent visiting among members of different communities and areas, larger and more frequent deliveries of products to local grocers, and more use of services outside the community. The coming of the automobile also seems to have encouraged earlier independence of young people.

In addition to automobiles and improved roads, the mass media have offered a window opening on the outside world. Education and literacy have increased, and with them readership of newspapers and magazines. Here in Shiloh, as perhaps in most places, Madison Avenue is a direct road to social change. As consumership is cultivated by corporations in search of expanding markets for products, tastes are changed, needs are created, old submerged wants are aroused, and motives for getting and spending are whipped up. Craig Bowman observed: "Standards of living have changed. Mountain people are more commercial-product minded than they were. That's partly the influence of television. Back then [in the 1940s] the only cereals a store had to carry were cornflakes and shredded wheat." Although the effects of television viewing and of radio listening can only be guessed at, the trends of ownership of the media instruments can be documented. In 1957, only 96 television sets were reported for tax purposes in the township, whereas about 270 sets were reported in 1965.[4] The number of radios increased from 79 in 1949 to about 170 in 1965.

Experience in the armed forces, in which many men have left the hills and have returned to tell of the outside, has also made available new standards and reference figures, new choices and decisions. Travel and letters and visits from migrant friends and relatives have had a similar effect. John Henry Sommers explained why he thought women in Shiloh were generally more dissatisfied with the way things were than men by saying that "the women of men who stayed here didn't have much when they got to comparing themselves to the ones that left." Craig Bowman's experiences away at college offer another example of how horizons in the valley have stretched.

[4] Of these tax listings, 197 were incomplete; however, a number of these listings are known to include television sets. Thus, 163 sets were listed, but there may have been as many as 360.

Largely because the mass media and improved communication and travel have offered a wider choice of standards and reference figures, divisions and differences appear between segments of the community which probably were not so pronounced in past decades. This subject goes to the heart of one of the major theses of this work—the existence of reference binds, or conflicts of values. One dimension of differences is that of age, as expressed by this lady's lament regarding the orientation of the younger generation:

> I think young people are more minded to the outside. Television has been a lot of that. Television is not all good, you know. It has stopped young people, and grownups, too, from reading. It's stopped some of them from going to church, too—they'll just sit home and watch some preacher on television.
>
> Now, cars, too, they'll keep young people on the roads. They don't stay at home at all like they once did.

Differences between younger and older generations show up in family situations and in the churches as well. The second important area of differences between segments of the community lies along the dimension of occupational type. The important differences in level of acculturation (into dominant American cultural themes) among different levels of families will be considered in this study.

Electricity, which made radio listening and television viewing possible in Shiloh, has come to the valley primarily during the last three decades. Electricity has also made possible the use of many appliances—stoves, refrigerators, freezers, clocks, vacuum cleaners, washers, lamps, furnaces—desired by many families. Indeed, electricity, and sometimes even a telephone, is installed in a house before bathroom facilities are brought indoors. I can recall visiting only one home that had no power, though many had no indoor bathrooms and some had no plumbing of any kind.

Telephones have existed in the community for many years, but there had been only three or four, scattered along the main road in stores or in the homes of the relatively well-to-do, until a short time ago. According to the county manager of the telephone company, one nine-party line extended up the valley as far as the Forest Service (several miles beyond Shiloh) before 1960; only four of these parties were in the study area. In 1963 there were 28 Shiloh listings in the telephone directory, and in 1965 there were 47 listings.[5] The manager estimated there would be approximately fifteen to twenty more telephones installed in the study area before the year (1965) was out,[6] and that the number would increase at rates like this as long as the company was able to extend its service and build new lines (the demand for telephone service is heavy).

Telephones serve as a communication link not only among local residents but between local residents and the outside as well, and in this way they serve the same window function as the mass media or visiting outside. One informant stated, for example, that the main use she intended to get from her telephone was to receive long distance calls from relatives who had migrated to Connecticut. Whatever their reasons, and whatever the consequences, most families are obtaining telephone service as it becomes available, and it will doubtless gradually become viewed as a necessity.

as mass media because of their importance as agents of

Schools must also be considered in the same category mass socialization of the young. Changes in schooling have been in the direction of consolidation, both on the

[5] Shiloh telephones are included in the larger Spartown exchange, and were extracted from the more complete listing by knowledgeable informants.

[6] By 1967, there were 69 listings.

grammar grade and high school levels, the former having taken place in 1951, the latter about seven years later. The multigrade, modern school that serves most of the valley's grade-school children is located in Shiloh; the high school, formerly located four miles from Shiloh, has been consolidated with other county schools in a new structure about ten miles away. Schoolchildren are interacting now with children from many different sections of the county instead of only with the neighborhood children, and they are being taught by a variety of teachers, most of whom live outside the community, instead of one teacher who often was also a neighbor. Increasing value is being placed on education by teachers, students, and parents, with the consequence that a higher proportion of students are finishing high school at the present time than in 1940.[7] According to the U.S. Census, the median number of school years completed in the county in 1940 was 6.3; the corresponding figure for 1960 was 7.7. Furthermore, the percentage loss in enrollment from the fifth grade to high school graduation has declined steadily from 69.6 percent in 1949–50, when earliest comparable figures are available for this dropout rate, to 39.9 percent in 1964–65. The difference in educational level between his own generation and today's young people impressed one informant so much that he remarked, "Only *one thing* I see has changed from when I was growing up is the young people are getting so much more education." He was not alone in noticing this change. Thus the schools increasingly provide windows and doors to the outside world.

All aspects of change in the area of mass media and

[7] See Berton H. Kaplan, "Social Change, Adaptive Problems, and Health in a Mountain Community" (unpublished Ph.D. dissertation, University of North Carolina, 1962), 140, where he cites an informant who says: "More folks around here came to realize that going to school was important. Talk to the most uneducated. They will tell you that going to school is important. They know how much it means to be without it today. The attitude has changed for many."

transportation appear to have the same net result. In general, the same things are happening in Shiloh that are happening throughout the rural Appalachian South: the frontier is passing away and a long period of relative isolation is over. As difficult as the process is to measure, it is nevertheless clear that the barriers to the outside drop away at different rates in different places, and it is difficult to say how Shiloh compares with other such communities in this regard. It is probably changing faster than some of the more rugged areas in West Virginia and Kentucky, but not as fast as the nearby county seat, Centerville.

While we are speaking of the community as a whole as though all members are affected by change alike, in truth, families located at different places in the community seem to have been touched and to have responded differently to the new experiences. The "isolation thesis" is really a misleading oversimplification, because the picture it connotes is one of an "inside," an "outside," and an impenetrable barrier between them that can be rolled down like a car window. In this analogy the barrier is physical and geographic—the mountains. A more accurate picture would play down the importance of the physical barrier and underscore the role of *cultural* barriers, which are like semipermeable membranes surrounding subpopulations. The permeable quality of these cultural membranes has always varied from one cultural subgroup to another in the mountains—some people have always been more susceptible to outside influences. Others, even though the physical barriers of the mountains have been overcome, have not been permeated greatly by the same outside influences, because their cultural membranes are thicker, denser. Consequently, the effects of reading, watching television, or attending school cannot be assumed to have a blanket effect of reducing isolation. To illustrate this point, Bud Blackburn's wife, who is not alone in her point of view, has "no use for science whatever," which she sees as a threat to real religion. Thus, she opposes much in contemporary education, and, when she sees articles in the newspaper regarding scientific achievements, she says, "I don't even strain my eyeballs to read them." In some cases, indeed, increased *cultural* isolation may result as a defensive mechanism in the face of decreased *physical* isolation. This more complex interpretation of the isolation thesis also allows us to reject the unreasonable assumption that mountain society was for some time completely cut off from the larger society, since anyone who knows Appalachian history knows that there have always been some travel and communication linkages, and that there has always been a segment of the population which has had contact with the outside world.

Perhaps no single area of daily life has changed so much since 1940 as that of work. Prior to the war, the economy of the Shiloh area was a mixture of subsistence farming, timbering, and mining. The gathering of evergreens was a secondary source of income, as it is at the present time. The need for cash was not so great then as now, and almost anyone could make a decent living from the land by cutting, digging, or planting it.

Some of the largest deposits of mica and feldspar in the United States are found near Shiloh, and the economic history of the area during and since the war is partly woven around the ups and downs of mining these minerals. Mica was used in bombsights and other military equipment during World War II. Since it was considered a vital material, government price supports were put under it and great quantities were purchased and stored in government depots. Mica mining boomed. Men and their families moved into the area for work, and a large propor-

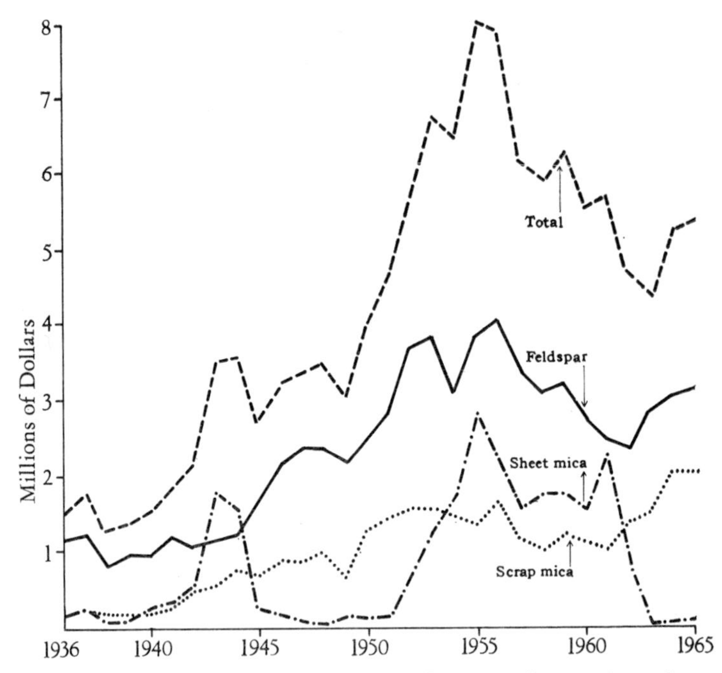

FIGURE ONE: *Separate and Total Values of Sheet Mica, Scrap Mica, and Feldspar Sold in the State, 1936–1965*

tion of the men in Shiloh were engaged in mining, processing, or transporting the material. When price supports were dropped after the war and there was no longer a guaranteed market, mining operations slowed considerably and many men were out of work. Then during the Korean conflict the government began buying again, and another, smaller boom followed. When the government mica program was again dropped in 1962, however, many men once more found themselves out of work, as wildcatters were forced out and the bigger companies slowed down.

Feldspar mining has also seen periods of increased and decreased activity, but the pattern has not been so irregular as with mica. During the study period fewer than forty men were employed by the two nearest mica and feldspar companies, and there were no wildcat miners. Since the end of the study period, the mica operation has been almost completely shut down and has sold out to another company, leaving fewer than twenty men employed (in feldspar, mostly). Of these twenty, only about six are from Shiloh.

Figure 1 shows the values of the various forms of mica and feldspar sold from 1936 through 1965 and underscores the economic instability of the industry, especially as regards sheet mica.

Looking at the percentage of white labor-force participants in major industry groups from 1930 to 1960 shows that the 6.2 percent in mining industries in 1940 fell to 4.2 in 1950 and 3.8 in 1960. (Unfortunately, such data cannot show the fluctuations that probably took place between those years.)

James Haskell still hangs onto mica mining as his main source of income, even though the plant he works at has been closed almost as much as it has been open during the past year. He and a friend describe what the mica business has been like from their point of view:

> Used to be able to make a good living at mining. When I started off years ago, it didn't take much money to set up. Labor was 50¢ an hour. Dynamite was cheap. Didn't have to settle the runoff [law requires this now to prevent stream pollution]. Only needed a mine and a couple of workers. You could sell it for $7.50 a ton. When I quit [running my own mine] about five years ago, labor was $1.00 an hour, dynamite was costing a lot, fuel was higher, the government and the state made you settle the runoff instead of just letting it run back into the stream . . . and I was only getting about $10.00 a ton.

> Yep. Mica mining's all over for the little man. Takes a big company now. They do all right; they'll be around a long time. [The plant closed and never went back to full operation after he said this.] You

> asked what it would take for a man to make a good living at mining nowadays. For an individual to make it, he'd have to have a good scrap mine (where you can pick up pretty good pieces without much work), a good water supply, and he'd have to be able to grind it. A man couldn't hardly do it. These flotation plants [a new, easy, but expensive way to separate mica from rock] is what's driving the little man off, too.

James, now in his fifties or sixties, came to Shiloh about thirty-five years ago from a little mountain community forty miles away. He says he had mined "in just about ever' miky mine around here; some spar, too." He quit trying to make it on his own and took this job five years ago. His younger brothers Howard, Henry, and Clarence followed him here and went into mining. Henry is now seasonally employed in construction, while Howard and Clarence are usually unemployed. Three other brothers also came, but they have left the mountains and settled in the nearby foothills with steady jobs. The glitter of mica was not gold.

Statistically speaking a more dramatic economic shift in Shiloh has been the shift from agriculture.[8] No one, to my knowledge, is now engaged in subsistence farming in the area. It survives only in small-scale gardening, in which almost every family engages. Commercial farming, too, is rare as a sole means of support: two dairy farms, one of which was owned by a nonresident; two cabbage patches, also owned by a nonresident; some cornfields, also owned by nonresidents; and one truck farm appear to exhaust the list. Some families raise corn or cabbage on the side as a cash crop, and many families tend small tobacco allotments for an extra bit of income.

[8] Shiloh reflects changes occurring throughout Appalachia, where agricultural and mining employment have dropped by 50 percent and 58 percent, respectively, from 1950 to 1960. See *Employment, Unemployment, and Low Incomes in Appalachia,* U.S. Dept. of Agriculture, Agricultural Economic Report No. 73 (Washington: Government Printing Office, 1965), 18.

The decline of agriculture shows up in a number of ways. The percentage of workers in the industry group of agriculture decreased steadily from 1930 to 1960 in the county from 65.99 percent to 24.65 percent. There has been a sharp, steady decline in acres harvested of all crops except hay and tobacco in the county from 1935 to 1962, from over 19,000 acres to 2,505 acres. Hay and tobacco are the only crops raised in any magnitude in the county now. The number of farms declined from 2,884 in 1939 to 2,154 in 1954. The percentage of the county's population classified rural nonfarm rose from 14.3 percent in 1940 to 57.9 percent in 1960.

Craig Bowman has his own index for the decline of farming in Shiloh itself:

> People don't farm like they used to. I'll tell you the best index of that is right here in the store—the amount of feed we sell. We used to keep a big amount of feed here and had to have it delivered every week. But now there's not nearly as many people raising beef, hogs, chickens, any kind of stock, and we don't sell nearly as much feed. Fertilizer, the same way. It shows up in the things they *do* buy. Milk, for instance. Everybody used to have a cow, and now instead of a big glass pitcher full, people pour it out of cardboard containers from the store. Eggs. We sell I don't know how many cases of eggs here a week. We've had to stock more meats, too, especially chicken. Yes, people need more money to buy these things with as they quit farming.

The need for cash may be part of the explanation for the decline of agriculture; it is increasingly difficult to live solely off the land. But the comments of several informants indicated that something else was also at work—a change of attitude or a change of value, perhaps. Farming is simply not "in" any more. I asked an elderly but outspoken lady, "Do you think it's harder to live off the land nowadays?" She said, "No, it ain't. The land gives you just as much as it ever did, if you know how to tend it. You can't starve. But the younger generation won't take up farming. They go to public jobs. They won't take hold of a plow handle for nothing." Perhaps what has happened is that the new economy introduces *prestige* into what before was merely a *subsistence* economy, as Abram Kardiner has suggested happened among the Betsileo when they shifted from a dry to a wet rice culture. Farming may never have been viewed in the mountains as a commercial enterprise, but as part of a way of life or a way of staying alive. If this were the case, one could as easily expect hunting and fishing to be converted into commercial activities as farming. More information is needed on attitudes toward farming before the problem of explaining its decline can be unraveled.

Timbering and sawmilling appear to have passed their biggest boom stages long ago, as the large, virgin stands have been almost entirely cut out. A state publication from 1896 describes the timber resources of the county at that time: "The walnut often attains the diameter of eight feet, wild cherry a height of sixty feet to the first limb, and with a diameter of four feet, the poplar with a diameter of ten feet, the black birch or mountain mahogany, the oak of several species, the hickory, maple, and ash, the yellow locust and other trees all of giant size. The quantity, magnitude, and excellence of forest stores has attracted attention from abroad, and large supplies are now annually cut, sawed and shipped."[9] "Paperwood" and smaller hardwood logs are still cut and sawed by several mills in the county, and members of several families in Shiloh are employed full time or part time in logging and sawmilling. These sources of employment and income are thought likely to remain fairly steady at the present

[9] North Carolina Board of Agriculture, *North Carolina and Its Resources* (Winston: M. I. and J. C. Stewart, 1896), 412-13.

level,[10] but this level is below what it was during the timber boom in earlier decades.

Census figures on employment in forestry are probably misleading because other related wood industries and fishing are included in the same category, but they show an irregular pattern from 1930 to 1960. Other data sources show fairly steady decreases in this section of the state and in the county with regard to number of sawmills, amount of lumber produced, value of sales, and employment from 1942 to 1964. The number of sawmills, for example, decreased from 747 in 1942 to 374 in 1957 in this section of the state. In the county, employment in the lumber industry dropped from 180 in 1958 to 75 in 1964.

With closeouts in farming, mining, and timbering as sources of employment and subsistence—trends occurring simultaneously with the whetting of new appetites for consumer goods and different life styles—many members of the community are turning elsewhere for sources of cash. Part-time commercial farming has already been mentioned. The gathering and sale of evergreens provides subsistence for some. The business of growing shrubbery (primarily boxwoods, laurel, punktatum, and rhododendron) and trucking them out of the mountains is growing steadily. The sale of land is another source of income; it is increasing with the growing tourist interest in the area.[11] The county department of public welfare is another source of cash for those who can qualify, as county data testifies. But the bulk of the working popula-

[10] Personal communication from a representative of the Forestry Division, North Carolina Dept. of Conservation and Development, Raleigh, N.C., April 1966.

[11] One tract of land (220 acres) was sold during the study period for $35,000. A "park" has opened on Yellowjacket with lots to sell to tourists. Craig Bowman and his father have purchased land for the same sort of development; individuals such as Howard Haskell and Guy Patrick have sold parts of their own property within the past two years to summer residents; the list could go on.

tion is turning to another relatively new source of work and money, and capitalizing on this new opportunity has brought about some significant new patterns of life in the community. This new source of employment is in the many mills and factories located outside the community.

Increasingly, both men and women are commuting to work outside the community—some, indeed, outside the mountains. Data compiled by the state mental health planning staff shows that in 1960, about 14 percent of the working population of the county worked in another county. Although this figure is not high when compared to the state average of 14.3 percent, it is high when compared to other mountain counties, only one of which has a higher rate. The figure may well be even higher for commuters from Shiloh itself, since some residents commute to work within the county but outside the community.

The term *commuting* usually means only leaving the community of residence for work in a different community, and we customarily think of it as a daily practice. It may make better sense to speak of commuting for a week, or a month, or several months for some purposes, particularly if this is the definition of the person doing the commuting. In Shiloh there are commuters who come home once during the week and on weekends, weekly commuters, and men who stay out for several months on a job before returning home. There is one point in common: all these individuals define the situation as working in one place but living in another.

Much of the new work is of a type that can be done by women as well as by men, and indeed, many women have joined the labor force since the Second World War. Percentages of female workers in major occupations for the county in 1940, 1950, and 1960 show that the largest gains are in white-collar and blue-collar occupational categories. For all occupations, the percentage female rose from 10.8 in 1940 to 14.4 in 1950 and to 25.4 in 1960. In some cases both husband and wife work at jobs outside the community; if their shifts happen to come at different times, they rarely see each other except on weekends. This is a radical alteration from the time when family timetables were scheduled around farm activities. This shift in employment patterns means that family members, whether husband, wife, or child, spend more time away from home and the home community compared to former times. Readjustments in family patterns are obviously required, and changes in attitudes toward performance of new roles are necessitated for smooth transition to new arrangements.

Another general trend in employment is an extension of the more basic trend toward employment outside the community of residence: full-scale migration. There is some problem in definition, in that it is not always clear where commuting stops and migration begins. Nevertheless, we might consider migration to have taken place when an individual moves his place of residence to his place of work outside the community. James Brown and George A. Hillery have documented the migration pattern for the Southern Appalachians as a whole with available census data and find that more than two million people left the region between 1940 and 1960.[12] Shiloh appears to have made its contribution to this figure. The county in which it is located lost 18.6 percent of its population, or 3,194 people, between 1940 and 1960. Census figures for total population in the county and the township are given in Table 1, where it may be seen that the population of the township also declined remarkably in the same twenty-year period. (The percentage decline was 18.4 for the township.) According to a state mental health plan-

[12] James S. Brown and George A. Hillery, Jr., "The Great Migration, 1940-1960," in *The Southern Appalachian Region: A Survey*, ed. Thomas R. Ford (Lexington: University of Kentucky Press, 1962), 34-78.

ning staff report, the county was one of the nine highest in the state in terms of net outmigration of all whites from 1950 to 1960 (six of the remaining eight are also mountain counties).

TABLE ONE: *Total Population of County and Township in Which Shiloh Is Located, 1940, 1950, 1960*[a]

	1940	*1950*	*1960*
County	17,202	16,306	14,008
Township	1,701	1,540	1,388

[a] U.S. Bureau of the Census, *Eighteenth Census of the United States: 1960. Number of Inhabitants, North Carolina,* 20.

It is not entirely clear who leaves, what the destinations are, what the reasons for leaving are, and what successes the migrants find when they arrive at their respective promised lands. The loss of young adults from 1950 to 1960 has been heavy (over 40 percent).[13] The points of migration for fifty-nine Shiloh families which Kaplan studied ranged from adjacent counties (42.3 percent) to nonsouthern states (25.4 percent), with the remainder of the state and the southern states absorbing the rest (15.3 percent and 16.9 percent, respectively).[14] These figures suggest that the destinations vary considerably. It is unusual to find a man in Shiloh who has not lived elsewhere for at least a short time, frequently, but not always, in towns and cities within 100 miles. Destinations in other states include New Hampshire, California, Connecticut, Indiana, Kentucky, Virginia, West Virginia, Maryland, and Pennsylvania.

Generally, there appear to be two types of migrants from Shiloh: extended visitors, who return home frequently after periods of residence elsewhere, and more

[13] North Carolina Mental Health Planning Staff, *A Comprehensive Mental Health Plan for North Carolina* (N.C. Dept. of Mental Health, Raleigh, 1965).

[14] Kaplan, "Social Change," 61.

permanent outmigrants who have more or less wholly transplanted themselves. The former type favors single men and the relatively unskilled, whereas the latter includes single men, some women, whole families, and the more highly educated. The transplants do not return home for extended periods of time, but they do maintain family contacts and return fairly frequently for short visits. It also appears from casual observation that in general the transient type migrants travel farther from home than do the more permanent transplants. An informant from a nearby county suggested that this was so, and further suggested that both patterns can be explained by the desire to maintain family and home ties, either by frequent short visits from nearby or by long visits home from distant points. Occasionally single migrants marry "on the outside." When this happens, the couple frequently does not return to Shiloh.

The most important reason for leaving Shiloh is uniformly given as the need for employment. Migrants who were interviewed, as well as those who stayed, recited the same chorus: "This is the greatest place in the world to live if you just have the means." Other reasons sometimes mentioned were curiosity and boredom, wanderlust, and the desire to get out from under the authority of the family. Referring to women who want to move out, John Henry Sommers remarked, "A lot of them don't want to stay around their parents; they want to have more responsibility and be more on their own." In the same conversation, his wife, Hope, commented that "some people want to see different places and different things." Thelma Flood describes what her husband, Roy, felt about his work on the outside, which offers a clue concerning his motives for leaving:

> He worked on the Great Lakes six or seven years. He worked there about four years before we got married, and then he went back afterwards for about three

> more years. I didn't go with him; I stayed here. I didn't like him working up there, it was so far away. I guess it's because I didn't like it that he came back. But I think he'll go back sometime, he liked it so much. He talks about how it was sometimes, and you can tell he really loved it. He has a picture of the ship he was on, with his bunk-room marked on it, and he takes more care of that picture than I would anything. I think he'll go back. He talks about the crew a lot. They don't keep up with each other, except this one man—he used to send a card every Christmas. There was a lot of Mexicans, and this one great big one was Roy's friend. Sometimes when they were off duty they would go down on the docks where a lot of bums hang around and they might try to hit you on the head and take your money. But they never bothered this Mexican and Roy.

It was clear, however, that few persons wanted to uproot themselves from this place permanently (though it is true that the individuals most desirous of being elsewhere probably already were). As one man said simply, "I've been a lot of places in my life, but I've never found Shiloh." There was a strong sense of loyalty, belongingness, or at-homeness, a feeling that was well expressed by a couple who said they had thought about moving out but decided they wouldn't be happy elsewhere. The wife was asked what she thought would make her unhappy living on the outside. She replied, "Well, it's the little things, things that make your way of life. We have old friendships, old family ties here that have meant so much to us. We would miss these. Of course, people outside are nice people, they probably aren't any worse than people that live here, but living outside just wouldn't be *home,* if you know what I mean. It's something I feel, but it's hard to put into words." Her husband added, "The way I feel, I was borned here and this is my *home.* I like to go to church here. It's just home." This strong sentiment doubtless has some important functions both for the migrants and for those left behind, primarily in reinforcing solidarity in the face of relationships broken by geographic and social distance, although this remains to be documented.

Aside from the effects on commuting and migrating to work and on family reorganization, the work itself is often a new kind of encounter for the people of Shiloh. More people are working for wages now than formerly, and more people are working for other people now, compared to 1940 when many worked for themselves in farming, timbering, and mining. Fewer jobs today are seasonal in nature or are affected by weather conditions. One man who is typical of the new category of factory workers has been commuting to work five and six days a week for ten years to a factory thirty miles away. He says he has seldom been late for work because of the weather and has never missed an entire day on that account. Another man has been with the same mill since it began operation sixteen years before. This pattern contrasts sharply with older forms of work, such as sawmilling, which slows considerably when the temperature drops in the winter.

The new work makes demands on attitudes, too. Factories run on timetables that are foreign to much of the older mountain culture, where time was marked by seasonal change, important events, and the length of shadows.[15] Rafe Franklin, currently unemployed, describes his experience working in a furniture factory: "Boys, they really made you work there. It wasn't that somebody was watching you. You couldn't goof off even if they wasn't or you'd be piled up. Them boards coming at you almost faster'n you could take them." Factory work in-

[15] See John Cassel and Harman A. Tyroler, "Epidemiological Studies of Culture Change: I. Health Status and Recency of Industrialization," *Archives of Environmental Health,* III (July 1961), 25-33.

volves supervision which, though not always lacking in older forms of work, were of a different, more informal, familial-paternal type. Another informant who was also "between jobs" said he quit his factory position because his foreman was always "pushing and pushing, always after you." The emphasis is now on turning out the product and making a profit, whereas in the past (and now in still-existing older work forms) this goal was frequently secondary to that of maintaining personal relationships. Jack Snyder, office manager of Northern Mica located in Shiloh before it was sold in 1966, was asked to give a concrete example of the independence of local workers. He said:

> No, I can't give anything specific; it's just an impression you get about people's attitudes. You know, some men from here work at construction other places and some of them when they make up their mind they like the man they work for will be hard workers and loyal ones. We've had contractors come back down here trying to replace ones from here that have left them, they're such good workers. But if they don't like you, they're just as likely to pick up and go home as not. It seems like a man's relationship to his work isn't so much an economic tie as a personal one to the man he works for. (Of course, economics counts some.)

Traditionally, work has been an activity carried on almost exclusively outdoors in Shiloh. Some men today apparently cannot tolerate indoor work. Vern Roberts had a good job at a blanket factory near a city 35 miles away, but he left because "I just didn't like sitting behind a key all day there. I wanted to get something more outdoors. They didn't overwork you there; it wasn't that. You could get by with doing nothing there easy; wasn't anybody looking over you all the time. I don't know what it was; just being indoors, I guess." For this reason, jobs in timber and especially construction are very popular. An interesting parallel may be drawn to the Hammonds' description of the industrial revolution in Britain, which brought many discomforts of the new discipline of factory work to a people unused to industrial rhythms. The Hammonds' observations on the industrializing British relate also to the residents of Shiloh: "In the modern world most people have to adapt themselves to some kind of discipline, and to observe other people's time-tables, to do other people's sums, or work under other people's orders, but we have to remember that the population that was flung into the brutal rhythm of the factory had earned its living in relative freedom, and that the discipline of the early factory was particularly savage. . . . we have to remember too that poor people rarely had a clock in the house.[16]

The impersonal quality of the new work extends to hiring and promotion policies, which are based more on plant needs and the individual's qualifications and less on personal and familial relations and obligations and the individual's personal history. This is true even in the case of a small mica company, such as Northern, which is not locally owned. Cited here is the record of a conversation I had with Jack Snyder:

> I told Jack this afternoon that Howard Haskell hinted around for me to hint around for a job for him at Northern. He had said, "I really would like a job. Sometimes it don't take much—if the right fella just says something to somebody. Somebody like Jack, now, if he was to say to Grinshaw [the superintendent] 'I think Howard would be a good worker, (etc.),' why I bet I'd have me a job in two weeks. They's always

[16] J. L. Hammond and Barbara Hammond, *The Town Labourer, 1760–1832: The New Civilization* (London: Longmans, Green, 1949), I, 33-34.

> some work that needs to be done, going from one place to another, even if all the regular jobs is filled."
>
> Jack said that Howard was a good old boy, and he would like to do something for him, but that they couldn't afford to hire a man that couldn't do a number of things. "Howard could do maybe one simple thing, but we need people who can do welding or repairing or something besides what he's hired to do. We have one boy that can't read or write, and we hate to fire him. But he gets in the way sometimes when something breaks down. You send him for a wrench of a certain size, and he brings the first one he comes to. We'll keep this boy on, but we . . ." [meaning he wouldn't hire any more like him].

Jack denies any nepotism in the company. Many workers are related to each other, but Jack feels this is not due to nepotism but to the fact that no matter whom you hired, some would be related. There are brothers, uncles, and nephews, fathers, and sons, father- and son-in-law. Two or three family sets, according to Ted, include most of the workers. Most of the factories and mills, of course, are still more rationally structured and bureaucratically inclined than this small mining company, and there is less opportunity for relatives to work together.

Noise, monotony, claustrophobia, and unhappiness with supervision are given by various informants as reasons for not liking factory work. One local story that has been handed down with embellishments over the years tells of a man who helped build the "scenic," a parkway through the mountains nearby. Although his was not a factory job, the story illustrates well one local attitude toward close work supervision. The man's job involved hauling loose dirt and rock away from a construction site and dumping it over a nearby cliff. After dumping each load, he would lean on his wheelbarrow and watch the dirt cascade to the bottom of the cliff. The supervisor, after watching the worker enjoy several episodes of this time-wasting spectator sport, walked over to him and said gruffly, "Why don't you get another and watch it chase the first one down?" To which the worker is said to have replied, "Why don't let's watch the *wheelbarrow* chase it?" At this he pushed the wheelbarrow over the cliff and "went to the house" (walked off the job).

These few examples of the demands of the new type of work are sufficient to show that what is occurring is a movement in the sphere of work from "folk" to "urban," *Gemeinschaft* to *Gesellschaft,* or whatever related continuum one wishes to apply. The examples given here imply that there are problems of adjustment to the new work. In fairness, it must be said that many persons seem to fit into the demands of the new work without any special problems—particularly women. In support of this observation there is the testimony of the manager of a plant that hires around two hundred workers from in and near the county: he reports no problems of morale or absenteeism and no special problems of supervision. He himself feels that the myth of mountaineer independence is overrated and finds that mountaineer millworkers are the same as millworkers elsewhere.

Such a general statement concerning the changing nature of work must be qualified in several ways. First, we are not certain that the urban frame of mind was totally absent in 1940; in fact, this seems unlikely. What seems to be occurring is an increase in the proportion of Shiloh residents who have significant contacts with urban situations. It may be that there is no absolute decrease in *Gemeinschaft,* but merely a relative increase in *Gesellschaft.*[17]

Second, it should not be assumed that all members of

[17] See Peter Carstens, "Anthropological Aspects of the Community," John W. Umstead Lectures in Community Mental Health (Unpublished paper, University of North Carolina, Raleigh, Feb. 1965).

this community at present have a large number of contacts with *gesellschaftliche* settings. A number of persons are still engaged in older forms of work. Not all those who commute and migrate travel to factory-type jobs, although it appears that the majority does. Some migrate to timbering and mining jobs, some commute to construction jobs, and though these jobs may involve wagework, supervision, and employment by a company rather than self, they still tend to retain much of the flavor of the older forms of work, since supervision is looser, work is seasonal, and the work groups tend to develop more personal relations and primary ties than factory work groups seem to. Moreover, a significant number (though probably not a majority) are still involved in the older work forms within the community, including such marginal occupations as galacking, unsalaried preaching, jackleg mechanic work, and shrubbery-growing. Some men maintain these as second occupations while holding down regular jobs in factories, or they may engage in regular wage labor for part of the year and take up a marginal occupation during the remainder.

It is also important to emphasize that some persons in the community have no gainful employment at all, but rely on family or outside agencies for financial support and the satisfaction of basic needs. The number unemployed, in fact, appears to be increasing. The report of the state mental health planning staff, for example, shows that the county in which Shiloh is located has had the greatest percentage loss in employed white males from 1950 to 1960. The rate for the county is minus 30.5 percent contrasted with the state rate of plus 4.3 percent. Furthermore, this is one of six counties in the state in which there are as many as twenty or more underemployed or idle white men for every one hundred in the labor force (the other five are also mountain counties). The same source shows that the county had one of the thirteen highest percentages of recipience of Aid to Dependent Children in 1963–64, between 8 and 9.9 percent (the state rate was 4.73 percent). The county ranks among the top nineteen in terms of the percentage of the population in the 16-64 age bracket receiving Aid to Totally Disabled Persons in 1963–64, or between 1.4 and 1.69 percent (the state rate was 0.86 percent). In terms of Old Age Assistance in 1963–64, the county ranked among the top twenty-one in the state—19 percent (the state rate in this case was 14 percent).[18]

For many of these non-self-supporting families, the demands of newer forms of work have not made themselves felt in the same way they are felt by the new class of millworkers and factory workers because the new forms of work have not reached them. Nevertheless, their economic situations are not unchanged from what they were in the past. On the one hand, there is more need for cash, and, on the other, there are more ways at present to get it, even without working: more agency programs and more tourists who will pay high prices for otherwise useless land, to name but two. Changes in the economy and the structure of work have left no one in Shiloh totally unaffected.

Other areas of change in Shiloh include religion, social and recreational activities, and patterns of social ranking.

There are two categories of church in Shiloh; they can be classified from a number of observable characteristics. From the theological doctrines espoused in sermons, hymns, and prayers, three of the seven churches would be classified as fundamentalist and the other four as relatively modernist. The fundamentalist churches are smaller and of lower property values than the modernist

[18] All figures cited are from the North Carolina Mental Health Planning Staff, *Mental Health Plan.*

churches. The fundamentalist churches are unaffiliated sect groups, whereas the modernist churches belong to regular denominational groups (two are Baptist, one Methodist, and one Presbyterian). The fundamentalist churches are located farther from main roads. Their preachers are not ordained, but are "called," frequently with little or no pay. The form of the fundamentalist service involves more participation, activity, and emotional expression than does the form of service in the modernist churches.

Members of both types of church remarked frequently about the increasing problem of keeping the young people interested. The young sometimes appear impatient with what they see as old-fashioned or backward ways of doing things, as this informant indicates:

> *Interviewer*: Do the younger people see things differently from the older people? I mean, do the younger ones tend to compare things to the outside where the older ones compare things with old ways of doing things?
>
> *Ollis Vance*: Now, I might have a hard time understanding you because I ain't had much education and ain't been around like some of these people. But if I understand what you mean, I think that happens—young people kindly think about outside and older people think about how things has always been. You can ask somebody like James Haskell about how things has changed in the church. Not too far back, a bunch of young people got up the idea of getting robes for the singers up at Three Knobs. James has been deacon up there for thirty years, I guess. He said as long as he'd been there they didn't need such as that, and he wanted things to be like they had been. He said he was too old to change now, and he was 100 percent again it. Said if the rest wanted to vote him down then that would be all right. But they went along with him. Yes, you can see that these young people

> has got some of this new religion and a different idea about worship and all. I'll stick to the old ways myself.

Another man, who had attended both types of church, said he had withdrawn because "there's too much friction in the church." Asked what the friction was about, he said that they argued over scripture and called each other names ("vilified one another"). "One says they're Baptists and another says they're Holy Rollers, and on like that. They probably all mean well, but I just don't want to get mixed up in it."

One faithful attender's explanation for the increasing lack of interest was theological in nature, but the man conversing with him had a more earthbound view:

> It's because the end is coming. There's a great falling away; that's what it prophesies in the Bible.
>
> A lot of people coming up now, like me, aren't interested in it any more. I'll tell you, back ten and twenty years ago, there wasn't anything to do but go to church. That's all anybody had they could do. Now, though, there's so many other things they can do instead of go to church, like getting in the car and going someplace.

Another reason why young people are not attracted to the church is implicit in Ollis Vance's remarks above: the young people are not able to take part in rewarding activities of the church, because it is structured in such a way that authority and prestige go with age. The older persons in the church, whether fundamentalist or modernist, are the leaders and decisionmakers. A lady in a Baptist church, for example, said that down through the years a small group of older ladies had kept the WMU (a Baptist women's organization) going, and that for a period of years she and one other older lady had met by themselves. When delegates were "volunteered" to represent their churches at state conventions, older persons were elected. Young "preachers" are offered the pulpit sometimes in the fundamentalist churches, and in all churches young people are encouraged to sing in front of congregations. However, with these exceptions, the young reap few earthly rewards for participation in the church as a social organization.

Whether the church as an institution is losing its centrality in the social life of the community is difficult to say. Expressed and observed difficulties in recruiting both young people and adults for participation in church affairs indicates that there exists today some serious competition for the time and energy of church members. One of the fundamentalist churches has difficulty finding a preacher for more than several months at a time, and the others depend almost entirely on spontaneous volunteers for preaching. The following entry in the field notes shows the difficulties one of the Baptist churches was experiencing in getting church groups organized:

> Toward the end of the service, Mrs. Bertha Harmon (widowed, about 65) rose to say something she had had on her mind a long time. There has been difficulty for many years getting people to attend and join the various auxiliary groups set up by the Baptist church: the WMU, YWA, GA, RA, etc. She pleaded for ten or fifteen minutes for more people to take an interest in these groups. She read a number of figures on the growth of Baptist mission work throughout the world since the war, and said that a small church like this should take pride in being part of such a large effort.

There was little response to her plea, at least during the remainder of the field visit.

Changes in forms of social and recreational activities,

again, can only be inferred, because there is no direct evidence from the past with which to compare the present. One can be fairly certain that the automobile has had considerable impact in this area of life [the number of cars reported for tax purposes increased over five times from 1949 to 1965 in the township]. As a 76-year-old widow who pictures herself as "an old woman settin' up thar on the mountain" said simply, "Cars changed more around here than anything." For most of the young people, cars are more than transportation (if somewhat less than the symbols of "emancipation from the old social order," which Tom Wolfe supposes them to be[19]); they are important forms of social activity, sources of pride and prestige, means of achieving independence.

It appears from informants' statements that most social activities in 1940 took place in the church or in the home. It appeared to one woman that "families don't do much anything together any more. We used to sing an awful lot together. We had good times together singing. Then a lot of times we would take turns reading. No one does that any more." Her husband broke in, saying, "No, everybody has to be in a different place, you see. Of course, back then there weren't any cars and roads, and there wasn't anything to do but stay at home and do things like that."

Visiting, as a pattern of social or recreational activity, appears to have decreased over the years, if informants' reports are to be trusted. One man says he doesn't visit other people because he talks to them all day in his business and doesn't want to be around them after work hours. Another man says he just doesn't have time to sit around and talk. Thelma Flood reflected at lunch one day that people don't visit now as they did in the past. I asked

[19] Tom Wolfe, "The Last American Hero is Junior Johnson. *Yes!*" *Esquire* (March 1965), 74.

her why she thought that was so. "Well, people are working out on the job all day, and then work around the house when they get home—I guess they just don't have time. There's a lot of women work, too. They wouldn't be able to visit as much. And a lot of the women that don't work, their husband has to have the car, so they can't get around to see anybody, especially if they have a bunch of children." My field notes also indicate that travel was not once such a problem, since friends, relatives, and neighbors lived closer to one another, but since transportation has improved, friends and relatives live farther away and visiting requires longer trips.

Telephones have also cut down on home visiting. The John Henry Sommers family lives a quarter-mile from his father's family, and neither of them had telephone service during the study period. Some member of one of the two families was on the road to one house or the other almost all the time—on the way to borrow, or babysit, or gossip. When I made a return visit in June of the following year, telephones had been installed at both houses, and the traffic between the two homes was observably lighter.

Nevertheless, informal visiting is an important social activity for many people, especially women. There are survivals of older forms of social activity among the men, too, in addition to church affairs, including fishing, hunting, drinking, and gambling. Cornhuskings, barn raisings, and quilting bees appear to be things of the past, although two new forms of collective recreation have taken their place in the past few years. One is the shower for brides and expectant mothers (which a few men as well as women attend). The second is the community softball team, which was spontaneously organized in the summer of 1965. Many able-bodied young men from all parts of the community (and all social levels) were drawn into the sport, and the team competed with similar teams from other nearby communities. Women's softball teams were also organized.

Regarding social classes or levels in Shiloh, few informants spontaneously drew attention to their existence, but they existed nonetheless. One of the few persons who seemed aware of differences in social level was a rather status-conscious informant who was himself in the top level. At one point he made a statement which many others had made, "We don't think too much in terms of social class up here." Later in the same interview he said jokingly, "There are four social classes here: the lower, the middle, the upper, and me." He also showed awareness of differences in social level when he observed: "Now, these other people like John Henry and Hope—they're mighty fine people—they'll get together with other people every night and sing or eat and visit. But we never go down there even though I know we'd be welcome, and I've never thought about having them up here." Another man who was aware of status differences was Charles Shores, who drew a distinction between factory jobs like his own ("gentlemen's work") and jobs like mining, logging, and farming ("grubbing").

Most informants did not mention differences in social level and tended to play them down when I brought them into the conversation. One schoolteacher, for example, responded, "That's one thing about this community, they isn't too many classes. Nobody makes distinctions here. Everybody gets treated just the same." Once the denial was made, however, all informants were able to offer examples of families who would be representative of a top, middle, and bottom level in the community. Thus, social levels do exist alongside the myth of their nonexistence. Local perception of these social levels indicates that the bases of social class are in the process of change. The root source of the change appears to be the increased occupational differentiation. Kaplan notes that in earlier decades most men were farmers: "Farming was the master occupational role; there was little choice."[20] As one key informant put it, "Most of our forefathers were more or less peasants when you come down to it, and there isn't any social structure among peasants." Another informant, Ernest Phelps, said more simply, that "people were more nearly the same," but he added that there were ranked differences among merchants, farmers, and galackers. Ernest also noted in the same interview, "I'm not sure what it would be today that counts. It's not too clear." This lack of clarity in the social structure is widespread, as Kaplan has documented, but the sources of change are evident enough for some informants to have caught a glimpse.

Eight bases for social ranking in Shiloh could be listed. I asked Craig Bowman, a shrewd if untrained analyst, to comment on whether they had changed since his early memories of the community (which would have been in the early 1940's). These bases for social ranking included land holdings, education, income, job, reputation (and personal characteristics), church, neighborhood, family, and politics. A few of his comments follow:

> *Land holdings:*
>
> This has changed as far as farmland is concerned, because there isn't as much farming. But I predict that land will be worth more and will be more important again in ten years.
>
> *Education:*
>
> There are probably more people with more education. It doesn't necessarily *mean* more, though. It probably meant more *then.*

[20] Kaplan, "Social Change," 123.

> *Family:*
>
> This still plays a part, but people are judged more on face value now. This is something that's changing in the whole country, not just here.
>
> *Job:*
>
> There is more variety in jobs now. They have changed from mine, timber, and farm then to mills today. This could well be more important now.
>
> *Income:*
>
> Income means less than the job, the kind of work you do. Two men might make the same and be ranked very differently.

More variety in jobs is also recognized by the local physician, who, when asked to describe social levels in Shiloh, chose occupation as the point of differentiation:

> Although there is much overlap, I suppose the lowest would be the galackers. Perhaps just above them come the timber workers. Then miners. Mining is a little steadier work than timbering, which depends on weather, but mining is going out and is not as steady as it once was. I suppose construction workers would come next; they are made up mainly of displaced miners. There are only one or two real farmers. Eph Greene is the only one I can think of that raises a cash crop. Then the textile workers, plant workers, they may be the most prosperous. They are about parallel to schoolteachers, except that the families of schoolteachers often have a double income. The merchants would also be at the top. Some of the storekeepers also have other interests and have a double income. Ernest Cummings is an example.

Doubtless this informant could have enumerated other occupations and finer shades of stratification; the number of ways of making a living in Shiloh today is surprisingly large. According to my notes of this interview, this informant agreed that occupation, income or wealth, and education were probably more important bases for ranking now, whereas property ownership (land), family name, and personal esteem were more important in the past.

A minister observed that education probably is more important today than in the past. I asked him and his wife to describe or name families at different levels in the community. As they were discussing families between themselves (I did not offer any names for discussion), they brought up such matters as amount of land owned, income, job. I don't remember any mention of education or family name per se. Occasionally (but not often) a personal trait was mentioned, such as drinking. Both the minister and Ernest Phelps, as well as others, mentioned the importance of income and money in social ranking today.

Thus, it appears that the bases for social ranking are shifting away from family name and toward occupation and income. The position of land ownership as a basis of rank is not clear, probably because the use and meaning of land has changed so rapidly. It is feasible that income is becoming more important as a point of differentiation, since it, like occupations, is becoming spread over a wider spectrum: the median income of families in the county increased from $1,212 in 1950 to $2,445 in 1960,[21] indicating that money is more plentiful in the county now than formerly.

Some informants are uncertain by what standards people rank other people today in Shiloh. They describe the strata as fluid:

[21] U.S. Bureau of the Census, *Eighteenth Census of the United States: 1960. General Social and Economic Characteristics, North Carolina,* 284; *Seventeenth Census of the United States: 1950. Characteristics of the Population,* II, Pt. 33, p. 135.

> *Interviewer:* Do you think it is meaningful to speak of three groups: a bottom, a middle, and a top?
>
> *Dr. Hertz:* No, I don't think so. It is too fluid. You can be affluent in one way and impoverished in another. And it is easy for a family to slip back a notch without really losing face.

Craig Bowman remarked, "The social structure is easy to move into and out of." His attempt in the same interview to describe the class position of a certain family demonstrates the nature of fluid strata and the essential lack of clarity in the ranking system:

> Herman Stevens is a good example of a man who has dropped from the upper to the lower. Maybe really to the middle, because he still keeps up appearances (his house), and he still has his family. That's a kind of backwards situation: his children pull him up instead of his ancestors!
>
> His children never were sure what social class they belonged in. They married different types of people—some with pretty good jobs and some more or less menial—and I remember back in school they had friends on both sides. I think Herman, Jr., will take his place as one of the most prominent people in Shiloh next year when he moves into his new place across from Lawrence Harmon's. One girl married a teacher who later became a school superintendent in another county, but she still has one of the lowest-paying jobs at the thread company. That's really mixed up, by gosh!

Difficulty in defining the local social structure is made worse for members of the community by the existence of a kind of double standard of stratification, in which both local and outside referents are used in determining rank. A social caseworker from the county seat did not even think there was an upper class in the Shiloh area; I therefore instructed her to think in terms of a top, bottom, and middle which would apply by local standards. This she was able to do, though with several comments like, "if you can speak of a top class." A minister said, "There aren't any [families] really at the top." He listed teachers, storekeepers, and contractors as the "fairly well-to-do," then added, "but even the top here is lower than outside."

Increasingly, the outside standard seems to gain in importance, affecting many areas of life. Ab Cooper tells how it has affected storekeeping: "Used to be that a storekeeper was as respected as a doctor would be. He had most everything a person needed and he could name his own price because he was the only one who had things people needed. Now you're in competition with a lot of other stores and with the towns."

To complete this overview of social change in Shiloh it is necessary to acknowledge that some areas of community life have not changed as much as others. First, it appears that in general what would usually be called "lower class" life is not changing as rapidly as life in higher community levels. Second, the area of political behavior does not appear to have changed significantly since 1940. Local politics still seem to be run by the "courthouse gang" in the county seat and their faithfuls in outlying districts. There is and has been no town government in Shiloh. People complain of politics in the schools. Vote-buying during elections has come to be expected:

> I'll tell you, this politics is so that an honest man wouldn't last long at it. It's something again. I was out here last year driving people to vote, using my own car to carry them in. I was using good Democrat

> gas, but we didn't have no money other than that last year. I saw this one man and asked him had he voted yet. He said he hadn't, nor his wife either, and I told them to get in the car right then and I would take them. You know what he said? Said, "Who's got the money?" . . . [He] said, "We ain't never voted without getting paid before. We always get about five dollars apiece." I said, "Well, why don't you just go ahead this time and vote anyways and see what it feels like to vote free."
>
> I tell you, it's just about any election, it wouldn't take but two or three hundred dollars to win it.

The political situation is and apparently has been very much as Paul Wager describes it for the Southern Appalachian Region as a whole: obsolete, machine-dominated, and based on a keep-taxes-low ethic.[22]

The political situation may be changing in some respects. There are several indications. Elections in the fall of 1966 were marred by the publicizing of voting irregularities such as underage registrations and illegal absentee balloting in the county. June 1967 saw a public, bipartisan meeting at the courthouse for the purpose of endorsing a change in the school board from appointed to elected—and therefore potentially multiparty offices. Cries of "politics in the schools" and "politics in the poverty program" are increasingly more insistent. More frequent are the assertions that people should vote for the man, not for the party. Even members of the dominant party are said to have switched allegiance in order to combat the stultifying effects of politics. Whether this is a permanent change of attitude, and whether it will produce practical, observable political results remains to be seen.

A third area of little change concerns the active involve-

[22] Paul W. Wager, "Local Government," in *The Southern Appalachian Region: A Survey*, ed. Thomas R. Ford (Lexington, University of Kentucky Press, 1962), 151-68.

ment of the community in county, regional, state, and national programs and organizations. Few members of the community are active members of the county chamber of commerce. Seldom is a county commissioner elected from this section. There are no civic organizations such as Lions and Rotary, nor any community improvement association—popular in many communities in the mountainous part of the state—nor voluntary associations of any kind. There is no community planning and there are no community-owned facilities. Outside governmental agencies involve themselves in the community (the Department of Public Health, the Department of Public Welfare, the Neighborhood Youth Corps, Friendly Home Visitors), but involvement of this sort requires no initiative or active response on the part of community members. Last, there are no communitywide social activities except the softball teams, which require minimal organization and are maintained only two or three months of the year.

II. *Families of Shiloh: A Typology*

The major goal of the fieldwork carried out in 1965 was to describe familial responses to crises that had been brought about by rapid social change. A secondary aim was to develop a typology of familiar coping patterns based on a knowledge of family characteristics, especially adaptive responses. Ultimately, the hope was that families which were successful in adapting could be differentiated from adaptive failures—whatever the specific ingredients of success and failure turned out to be—and that the latter might in some way be found associated with the production of illness. These goals were modified somewhat during the course of the field experience.

For one thing, the concept of crisis was found not to be a productive concept with which to work. Change in Shiloh, as experienced by its residents, has been gradual for the most part, and adaptation has been a slow accumulation of minor modifications rather than a sudden drastic reorganization of life. As Thelma Flood remarked when asked the kinds of problems that worry people like her: "I don't know. It's hard to think of them. Once you get them solved, you don't think about them any more." Craig Bowman, when asked about changes that had occurred in families, said: "That's hard to answer because things like that change so slowly you don't notice them. And it's something you wouldn't pay any attention to unless somebody like you asked about it!" If I could not study crises directly, however, I could at least watch daily rounds of activities, see minor problems handled by various family members, and listen to descriptions of past problems and their solutions. From these, I could begin to build pictures of adaptive styles on which a typology of families might center. The development of such a typology has grown into a major theme around which to organize observations of families.

Observations of a number of families and family members were recorded during the course of the fieldwork. At the end of the data-collection period, information from a variety of families had been recorded in the following areas (categories were set up about halfway through the progress of the fieldwork):

a. Occupation or means of livelihood
b. Social level in the community
c. Relationships to neighborhood and wider social contexts
d. Relationships to churches
e. Relationships to peer groups
f. Reference standards and figures
g. Resources for adaptation and their usage
h. Family structure
i. Value orientations

The data are limited in many respects. Information is not complete in all categories for all families. Since no standard schedule was used, not all persons were interviewed over the same range of topics. The typology resulting from use of available data, then, is part conclusion from the data and part hypothesis. It must still be regarded as an open question whether characteristics of families cohere in the precise manner and to the extent that is here suggested. On the other hand, I am not attempting to generalize about all mountain communities, nor about all families in this one community, but, rather, adducing data for the construction of types. If the data are limited, then so are the statements that are built on them.

It is impossible to generalize to any extent about *the* modal family in Shiloh. Perhaps a brief visitor would have less trouble describing a modal family, but one who stays long and is at all observant becomes sensitive to contrasts among families. There is, for example, the family of Ernest Phelps, store owner and Sunday school superintendent, whose life goals are modest but who feels pushed and hurried and thinks time may run out on him because of his heart condition. His attractive wife and four children, ages nineteen to four, would be the envy of any urban middle-class family man. They exude quiet respectability.

How different from the lively, grimy nest of Zack Painter, galax-picker, drawer of welfare checks, and self-made expert "called" to explain the book of Revelations. Here the Painters have spawned ten handsome, dirt-encrusted children, ranging in age from 13 to six weeks. The Painters, although they live on the periphery of the social life of the community, make their lives meaningful by sewing them into the fabrics of God and family.

Then there is the family of Henry Haskell who has mined, worked in timber, "followed construction," and "carpenters sometimes," who believes the earth is flat and, after a reckless youth, is a born-again Christian who won't go to movies or watch television because "that's the fakest thing they is." Henry's household includes his wife and two daughters, but it is really binuclear, like an amoeba undergoing mitosis, with his father-in-law's household next door forming the adjacent cell and the wife, like a piece of vital cellular material, shared by both.

There is Charles Shores, who commutes daily to a fiber plant thirty miles away with his wife and one of his daughters, where they all work on the third shift. Charles lives in a respectable white frame house and parks two almost-new cars beside it. One girl has finished high school, the other will finish soon. Charles quit mining and went to work in the factory years ago, and he enjoys the gentility of the new job which allows him to wear sports shirts and dress shoes to work. Since he quit "grubbing" he has little to do with his brothers and they no longer have anything to do with him.

There is Otis Graham, retired at 50, whose wife works at a mill in a nearby town. Otis raises the children while his wife supports the family.

There is Dave Norman, who commutes twice weekly to distant points and whose wife commutes daily to an office job in a nearby town—a couple who rarely see each other even when they are in town simultaneously because Dave has to see to his coon dogs.

There is Clyde Harmon, who likes the steady income of the factory job and submits to its routine without complaint, but who in spite of his own regard for future planning is raising a family of dropouts and drifters and teenage brides.

There are the families of Floyd Greene and Troy Stevens, who, despite just noticeable differences in accent and attitude, could pass for middle-class members of the environing, nonmountain society. There seem, in a word, to be as many different kinds of families as there are points on a compass or needles on a pine bough.

The family typology is ordered about variations in ways families have solved the economic problem, which appears to loom large as an adaptive problem in the community. Indeed, the problem of making a living was expressed in interviews and conversations more frequently than any other. The most typical expression of this problem was given by Sal Conway, when I happened to remark to him that this mountain community would be a good place to settle in: "Yes, it is—if a man has some means to live on. There are a lot of poor people living around here. Jobs are hard to find." Clarence Haskell, sitting in the shade tying galax leaves into bundles of twenty-five (each bundle worth 2.5¢), said, "This is an awful way to make a living, ain't it? But with jobs so scarce they ain't much else a fellow *can* do." The way Ernest Phelps expressed the problem was this: "What we need here is some kind of industry, some kind of small industry that would bring in a payroll. There's no payroll here now. Northern Mica doesn't hire many. Lumbering is about through. We need something that will bring some jobs." The solution to this economic problem—finding "means to live on"—is related to a host of other familial and personal characteristics and adaptive problems.

The economic problem amounts to deciding how one is going to secure what are defined as the necessities of life: food, shelter, clothing, medical care, or whatever else might be defined as necessary. For all families in Shiloh this means finding some kind of access to cash or credit (and credit must eventually be backed up with cash). Even in such a small community as this, an amazing variety in ways of acquiring cash can be found, including the following: working in mills or factories, mining, timbering, sawmilling, raising shrubbery, picking galax, social welfare and other agency support, dairy and truck farming, hiring out as unskilled labor, secretarial work, schoolteaching, pawning, newspaper distribution management, work with the state highway department, service station work, retirement pay, trading, preaching, bootlegging, chairmaking, gambling, sale of timber from own property, truck driving, working for antipoverty groups, selling newspapers, borrowing from family or friends, selling eggs and small quantities of produce, selling insurance, and selling votes.

This surprising variety reduces to a comprehensible order if we categorize families on the basis of whether most necessities are secured through:

1. full-time, year-round, nonseasonal, wage, or self-employment by the head of the household, including

managerial and white-collar jobs and ownership of a business (such as a grocery store); or

2. full-time, year-round, nonseasonal, wage, or self-employment by the head of the household in blue-collar work, including factory and millworkers and ownership of a small business such as trucking; or

3. fairly steady, usually seasonal, usually wage or self-employment by the head of the household, including the steadier semiskilled and unskilled workers in timbering, sawmilling, mining, part-time farming, carpentry, and construction (not at master level); or

4. occasional, little, or no real occupational engagement at all. This category includes families in which no members work steadily in the usual sense and who depend on agency support to a greater degree than other families. It also includes families whose members engage in sporadic, seasonal, unskilled, low-pay work such as galax-picking, farm labor, and other odd jobs, and unskilled mechanic work.

These categories of types of work are not as tight as might be desired, for there are some jobs that do not clearly fit into a single slot (e.g., farming is of various sorts), and the occupations of all family members are not considered—only that of head of the household. Nevertheless, the classification does include most normal households and allows them to be sorted on a dimension that is related to other characteristics. For example, it is related to subcultural orientations and values, in that the third and fourth categories include most older forms of work, and the people engaged in them are more enmeshed in a traditional way of life, whereas the first two categories are in most cases newer forms of work, and the persons engaged in them are more oriented to ways of life on the outside. One might well quote Herbert Gans here, when he says, "Although I have used occupational labels to distinguish between the major subcultures, a man's job does not necessarily determine in which of these he shall be placed. In the long run, however, the existence of a specific subculture is closely related to the availability of occupational opportunities."[1]

This classification of economic solutions is also a kind of occupational scale which, like occupational scales in other communities, could be used as an imperfect indicator of social class or level in the community.

Though not synonymous with social class or level in the community, occupational type is one indicator and is recognized as such by many members of the Shiloh community. For example, Dr. Hertz, the local physician who has been a perceptive observer of the community since about 1937, reluctantly consented to impose a three-group social class schema on the community in one interview. In doing so, he used occupational type as an indicator: "One might speak of a group which is permanently employed, many of which are in public jobs. Then those who are less permanently employed—those in timbering, mining, construction. And then those who are self-employed when they take a notion."

Kaplan speaks of the existence of three status groups in Shiloh: the "better" class, the "get by" class, and the "sorry" class.[2] I also used a three-level breakdown, partly because I was influenced by Kaplan's findings and partly because the number seemed natural to respondents and was conveniently small. Informants were simply asked if we might not speak in terms of three levels in the local community—top, middle, and bottom—and they were asked to suggest some representative families at each level. (It would have been possible to ask them to use two, four, five, or any other number of levels.)

[1] Herbert J. Gans, *The Urban Villagers* (Glencoe, Ill.: Free Press, 1962), 249.

[2] Berton H. Kaplan, "Social Change, Adaptive Problems, and Health in a Mountain Community" (unpublished Ph.D. dissertation, University of North Carolina, 1962), 70-75.

The six informants who were asked to suggest representative families at each of the three social levels were themselves of professional, middle-class, or upper-middle-class status. Included were schoolteachers, ministers, a physician, a welfare caseworker, and a public health nurse. All but one schoolteacher were marginal to the community in the sense that they either did not live there, had been away for most of their working lives, or did not identify themselves with the community, but they were nonetheless knowledgeable of the study area. These informants were thus considered to be good judges of stratification, although possible class bias stemming from their higher status position must be kept in mind.

The results of this procedure showed that although the relationship is not always perfect (meaning that social level is not identical with occupation), one would not be far wrong if he maintained that families with a certain type solution to the economic problem will be members of a certain social level. (It must be kept in mind that these social levels, like the categories of economic solution, have been somewhat arbitrarily forced into a particular number of choices.) The relationship between solution to the economic problem (occupational type) and social level is summarized in Table 2.

TABLE TWO: *Relationship between Occupational Type and Social Level in Shiloh*

Family Type	Solution to Economic Problem	Social Level
I	Full-time employment: managerial, white-collar, own business, etc.	Top
II	Full-time employment: blue-collar, semi-skilled, wage-worker, etc.	Middle
III	Fairly steady employment	Bottom
IV	Sometime or no employment	Middle

If other indicators of social level were to be used, the net result probably would be roughly the same. For example, an informant once happened to mention that the nicest houses in Shiloh belong to three families that would be listed as belonging in the top level. Furthermore, there is a tendency for residences of people in certain social levels to be located in the same neighborhoods, though the pattern is far from uniform. The three houses just mentioned, for instance, are clustered in the same neighborhood, along with other homes of families in or near the top level. Certain types of homes are grouped along the main road more than others; these tend to be homes of top and middle families. Other homes at the middle and bottom levels either cluster at points away from the main road or are strung out along backroads. Thus, social level is expressed in part ecologically.[3]

There are other matters such as relationship to churches and espousal of certain values which also could be considered related to social level and, indeed, often are. But they are important in their own rights as means of describing the relationships of families to their community environments and as ways of describing the internal makeups of families.

A word needs to be said about why the concept of "family type" is chosen over that of "social level" or "social class" as a way of organizing data from Shiloh. The imperfect relationship among factors such as perceived social level, occupation, neighborhood, and value orientations is of some importance in itself. It indicates that a social class conception of the social structure of Shiloh is too tight and too simple—as informants tried to express it when they said the class system was "fluid." Status differences are recognized; of this there can be no doubt. But other important types of differentiation are recognized

[3] Some local residents are aware of this ecological pattern: "If you took all the houses with driveways directly to the highway, they would all be in about the same class." "You could take the people at the head of upper Silver Creek, at the bottom of lower Silver Creek, on the upper Yellowjacket, and Dobbins Creek—they would all be about the same."

as well, and they are not reducible to social class, as tempting as this interpretation may be. My feeling is that the concept of class has been overused by sociologists, who employ it frequently to explain things it really does not explain. Thus, to announce that values, for example, are a product of social class is only to say that there is a tendency—and no more—for values and income level or occupation to cluster. As sociologists we are now just beginning to focus on the exceptions to the rule in studies of status inconsistency or incongruence; these studies may force us to reflect on our traditional conceptions of class and may make us hesitant to ascribe to it all the power and significance now attributed to it.

Because I hesitate to order the present data under the umbrella of social class, I have chosen to use the more neutral approach of the typology. All the typology says is that there is a tendency for certain characteristics to cluster. Perceived status level is one of these characteristics, occupation is another, and values another. There appears to be no theoretical or empirical reason to give any one of these dimensions conceptual ascendancy over the others. Thus, this is not just another stratification study, even though social level is one of the variables described.

There are several ways in which families can be described in relationship to neighborhoods. The social and ecological pattern just described constitutes one. Here I am concerned with a rough continuum describing the degree to which the family lives its total life within neighborhood confines as opposed to having significant contacts outside it. This continuum has been described by Godfrey and Monica Wilson as "scale": "the number of people in relation and the intensity of these relations." Another aspect of relationship to neighborhood not necessarily covered by the scale concept is the degree of integration of the family into whatever ongoing social life exists in the neighborhood. The research yielded no quantitative data to allow convincing demonstration, but there appear to be different patterns among families with regard to these aspects of neighborhood nonetheless.

If families are referred to by the type number (I, II, III, and IV) introduced in Table 2, it appears that, generally, neighborhood is of relatively less importance for Type I families than Type II, and for Type II less than Types III and IV. Many significant contacts for Type I families are with people outside the neighborhood, extending to the whole community, the county, or perhaps even larger social systems. Storekeepers talk to their wholesalers; contractors build houses outside the area; people speculating on land or investing in other businesses stay in contact with lawyers and bankers in the county seat; and entrepreneurs emphasize the need for cooperation on higher levels than family and neighborhood.

The families that have been labeled Type II appear to be more divided in their contacts between the neighborhood and beyond. Their work frequently takes them beyond the neighborhood and the community; though sometimes they will commute to work together, they seldom work side by side. Their friends might come from the neighborhood, but frequently they come from elsewhere in the community or vicinity. Type III families have a somewhat greater proportion of their significant contacts in the neighborhood, but, again, they often work with people from other communities, some of their friends come from elsewhere, and their children go to school with children from other locales. Type IV families seem to have the lowest proportion of significant contacts outside the neighborhood; they are not truly isolated, but, if this term is used in a relative sense, they are more cut off and self-contained than any of the other types.

The same picture emerges when one looks at the integration of families into neighborhoods. Where the families of Type I live there are few neighborhood activities, except for some visiting among relatives, and thus there is little for them to integrate into, as indicated by this excerpt from the field notes: "The Greenes do not seem to visit much in their own area or neighborhood. She visits her sister and her mother, among others, and when I came by last Monday night they were visiting a couple who have retired here from New York." There are no neighborhood churches in this category. Social and recreational activities (dances, parties, plays, meetings, vacations) are usually found outside the neighborhood or community. Type II families on the whole seem to be a little more neighborhood-oriented than Type I's, but there is little substance for them to be part of. Again, their important contacts outside the neighborhood probably take them into other parts of the community and the surrounding area for social activities. Type III's do more visiting within the neighborhood, and many of them attend neighborhood churches. Borrowing among neighbors is also commoner among Type III's, as it is also among Type IV's. Labor is borrowed, especially during tobacco-hanging season, tools, money, food, cars, car parts, guns, fishing gear, babysitting services, medicines, and sanitary facilities are borrowed year-round. Type IV families, like the others, frequently cross neighborhood lines, but there seem to be more neighborhood activities for them to be enmeshed in. For example, galacking groups tend to be made up of people from the same neighborhood. Churches and church activities tend to be located in the neighborhood, although there is frequent visiting from other neighborhoods whenever there is a church service or a "singing." Visiting between homes in Type IV neighborhoods appeared to be frequent, and neighborhood recreation, such as pitching horseshoes, also appeared more frequently among Type IV's. Children of these families attend school less regularly and tend to drop out earlier than children from other type families, therefore spending more time with children from neighboring homes and less with school activities and children from other areas. On one late Sunday night coonhunt, a boy of about twelve years accompanied the group. I asked the boy if he planned to attend school the next day and was told that he probably wouldn't, for he would be getting home too late that night and hadn't done his homework, having spent the entire evening before the hunt in a revival service. We emerged from the woods at about 1:30 A.M.

It must be noted that these are impressions not uniformly applicable to all families in the four general types. One important exception is in the Type IV category, where there are two distinct subtypes: members of the one subtype are rooted in a neighborhood and do not move from it, and members of the other subtype are the drifters, who move from house to house and neighborhood to neighborhood whenever the notion strikes them or when they are forced to move. Furthermore, neighborhoods in the community vary in the degree to which they can be called true neighborhoods; none is the self-contained unit of communal life it once is said to have been.[4] It can be said, nevertheless, that relationship to neighborhood varies roughly with family type in terms of scale and in terms of integration of families into neighborhood. Families toward the bottom of the scale of family types tend to live a greater proportion of their lives and be more

[4] For a discussion of social change in rural neighborhoods and different families' responses to neighborhoods, see John H. Kolb, *Emerging Rural Communities* (Madison: University of Wisconsin Press, 1959), esp. Chap. 4. He finds differences between "neighborhood families" and "non-neighborhood families."

enmeshed in activities of their immediate locales than those toward the top.

There are two basically different types of churches in Shiloh. It has been said that there are social-level implications of church membership and that certain of the churches are neighborhood institutions. That churches are related to social levels is suggested by one informant's referring to lower-status residents generally as "Freewill Baptist types." The exact denomination of the fundamentalist churches is not clear even to their members. Some refer to the churches as Freewill Baptist, others as Missionary Baptist, others as Holiness. One of these churches was even attended by a Mennonite family, indicating that the basic theology is shared by many fundamentalists under different labels. There is considerable divisiveness within these churches, some of it involving labels, some of it doctrinal disputes, some of it personal animosities. The informant observed, furthermore, "One thing you'll notice here is that anytime one of the Freewill Baptists get money, they move up to the [Silver Creek] Baptist Church." This observation is consistent with Thomas R. Ford's finding for the Southern Appalachian Region.[5]

More than one pattern emerges when we look at family relationship to church. There is the question, first, of where families of different types attend. Second, there is the question of which sex takes leadership roles in the churches. Third, there is the matter of describing the attitudes of different families toward church and religion in general.

[5] Thomas R. Ford, "Status, Residence, and Fundamentalist Religious Beliefs in the Southern Appalachians," *Social Forces*, XXXIX (Oct. 1960), 41-49. See also James S. Brown, "Social Class, Intermarriage, and Church Membership in a Kentucky Community," *American Journal of Sociology*, LVII (Nov. 1951), 232-42.

No Type I families attend fundamentalist churches, and only one Type IV family attends a modernist church regularly (actually, the wife attends one and the husband another). One Type IV man visited a modernist church once during the summer, and another man was seen in a fundamentalist church one night and in a modernist church the next morning, but these were exceptions. Type III families appear by and large to attend fundamentalist churches. Type II families, on the other hand, show no clear pattern, some attending one type church and others attending the other. That this level might be the point of crossover from Freewill Baptist to Silver Creek Baptist is suggested by the example of a man who moved up to a Type II job and who joined the Silver Creek Baptist Church, having been raised in a fundamentalist neighborhood church. In fact, even as a member of the new church he still carried the morally restrictive notions of the fundamentalist doctrine, even in the relatively free atmosphere of the other church. Perhaps significantly, this man has rejoined a Freewill church since the study period.

On the matter of leadership roles in the church, women hold a greater number of positions in the modernist churches than in the fundamentalist churches. Women in the fundamentalist churches can play active roles only in providing food for church dinners, leading Christmas programs, singing in choirs or quartets, occasionally offering testimonies, or "getting the spirit." For example, on one Sunday in June:

> A new group got up to sing, then, and while they were singing the "preacher" exhorted all those who had not been saved to come and be saved now, before it was too late. He told us not to let the Devil hold back God's spirit in us. Then another man got up during the singing and said, "Let's have a good old-fashioned handshaking! Everybody join in! Come on up and shake everybody's hand in fellowship!"

> Everybody (including myself) did indeed get up and drift to the front of the room. Everybody was shaking hands and some were bear-hugging each other, and the singing got louder, and people started wiping their eyes. I had gotten about two benches up from where I was sitting, when I was stopped by an earsplitting scream. The lady who had cried and given testimony earlier while singing began to cry and holler at the top of her lungs. Then another, older lady, who was being hugged by a young boy of twenty-odd, starting in shouting for Jesus. The whole place went mad at that; hands were pumping, bodies were squeezed, tears ran down cheeks, and people with glazed expressions mumbled, "Praise God, praise God, praise God."

But there are no female deacons, no women in the amen corner, and no women in the making of decisions concerning when revivals are to be held and what the money is to be used for, since it is said that "women should keep silence in the church." Women in the modernist churches, on the other hand, offer closing prayers, head up circles, Sunday school classes, and other church groups, serve as delegates to denominational conventions, and play a guidance function in church affairs.

Part of this difference can be accounted for by the difference in roles of women between lower and higher status families; the fundamentalist church, like the Type III and Type IV families, is ostensibly patriarchal, as is revealed by the following conversation I had with Howard Haskell and Brenda Douglas (young, Type IV, separated mother of two):

> I asked them at one point if they thought women were more bossy and wore the britches in the family more now than they did when they were growing up. Brenda said she definitely thought they were. How-

> ard agreed, and he was quick to add that his wife wasn't that way—she'd do anything you tell her and never talk bad to anybody, or if she did, she'd apologize.
>
> Brenda said she thought women were getting more say in the church, that you could see the difference there. Howard again agreed, and pointed out that the Bible explicitly states that women should keep silence in the church. "If they want something explained to them, they should keep their mouths shut and wait 'till they get home and ask their husbands." Brenda wondered, "What do you do when your husband don't know nothing about it?"

The structure of the denominational churches also allows for more female leadership because it includes more peripheral church groups such as Sunday school classes and missionary societies. Last, part of the leadership differences appears due to a combination of greater male recalcitrance and female aggressiveness (in the modernist compared to the fundamentalist churches). When the minister in a modernist Baptist church asked for volunteers to go as messengers to the state association and got two female volunteers out of a congregation of seventy, he asked if there weren't any men who could go; he appointed the women when he got no response.

In the home it is a different matter among the fundamentalist churchgoers; after all, the Bible only says women should keep silence in the *church.* In the home men may still have the final authority in interpretation of scripture and in the solution of ethical, moral, and theological problems, but women contribute considerably to the discussion. More important, it seems to be the women and not the men who keep religion an active daily concern. It is as though the women (and a few exceptional men who would be known as "preachers" and "saints") maintain religion, while the men merely run the church.[6] These observations do not apply so well to families attending the modernist churches, where men and women tend to exercise the same religious roles outside the church as inside, relative to each other. In these families, either may take an active role in church, and probably neither will make much of religion during the week. There are, of course, exceptions, but the typical case is that of the young man, a Sunday school officer at the time, who was overheard swearing at his father. When his attention was called to the apparent inconsistency, he replied that he was "only in church on Sunday, and I don't do things like that there."

The third area concerning the church centers on attitudes toward church and religion. In general, there seems to be a tendency for modernists (Type I families and some Type II's) to give religion and the church a less central place in their lives than do the fundamentalists (Type III and Type IV families and other Type II's). But this broad generalization covers only the churchgoers.

In all family types there are a number of persons who do not attend church. Attendance figures cannot be enumerated but my impression is that a greater proportion of Type I family members are regular attenders, and that men from Types III and IV families are the least regular, although women outnumbered men at all services I attended, regardless of church.

Religion as a whole appears to be less central to men than women and, despite impressions from sheer atten-

[6] It is uncommon to find fundamentalist gospel songs with themes about fathers, but there are innumerable songs about mothers. "My Mother's Bible" was once sung at a fundamentalist church in Shiloh and dedicated to all the fathers on Father's Day; comparable songs about fathers were apparently lacking. Other mother-theme gospel songs include: "If I Could Hear My Mother Pray Again," "Shake Hands with Mother Again," "Tell Mother I'll Be There," "Heaven Is Nearer Since Mother Is There." The significance would seem to be that women are more important bearers of religious culture than men among the fundamentalists. On the other hand, fathers may be omitted from mention because of potential confusion with the father-symbol of the Christian God, but there is no evidence on this point.

dance, that it is less central to families near the top of the scale of types.

Herbert Gans has underscored the importance of the peer group in the lives of Italian inner-city dwellers in Boston, demonstrating the influence of peers even in adulthood.[7] Jack Weller has applied Gans' finding to the West Virginia mountaineer and sees a striking parallel between the two cases.[8] However, Weller overlooks the fact that Gans' West Ender peer society is made up of both sexes, and he also generalizes the peer phenomenon to all types of mountain families. Observations made in Shiloh show that the peer group is likely to continue in importance into adulthood primarily in the cases of Type III and Type IV families, and then more among the males than the females within these types. Peer groups form in childhood, persist through adolescence, and continue into adulthood: "Usually I have seen Wade Harmon around town loafing with a bunch of other boys around his age [14-15]. They swim, ride around in cars, go to town, or stand or sit around talking and laughing." Usually, they loaf at one of the stores. Jack Snyder commented, "If you just spent one day in this office [next to a store] you'd see what they do all day long—tear up and down the road in cars or loaf at the store. I guess this is the place where most everybody loafs." I later observed and recorded this: "Eventually another boy dropped by the store and Larry talked him into going to Riverview with him. (Decisions like this are well thought out by the store gang. Yesterday it took an hour for five boys to decide whether to go in swimming or not, and another half-hour to decide where to go. They ended up not going. By 'boys' I mean anybody from 16 to 35 [or older?] years of age.)" Men

[7] Gans, *The Urban Villagers,* esp. Chaps. 4 and 10.

[8] Jack E. Weller, *Yesterday's People* (Lexington: University of Kentucky Press, 1965), 78-81.

and boys also spend a good deal of time at one another's houses. They hunt and fish together, drink, gamble, look for work, and migrate out together.

For the adult male toward the lower end of the scale of family types, "the boys" constitute an important social arena that competes with the family for his time, energy, and money. The rest of the family must accustom themselves to seeing the head of the household leave the house with friends as soon as he comes home from work or instead of going to work. Occasionally peer group influences suddenly cease around middle age, and a man settles down with his family, but the homebody type of adult male is not the only modal one in families toward the bottom of the scale, where the call of the peer group is strong. This reformation can occur at any age, but generally it seems to occur later among III's and IV's than among I's and II's. These field notes from 1967 offer a suggestive glimpse of early middle age metamorphosis in a Type III, John Henry Sommers:

> John Henry acts strangely tired. He suggested we take a nap instead of knocking around this afternoon—very unusual. He fell asleep watching TV at 4:30. Usually he wants to be up doing something. He was not even intent on his fishing today, though it is true the rain dampened all our spirits.
>
> Today he said about his age, "A man used to be proud to say his age when he is 26, 28, 29, but after you get past that 30 you don't feel that way no more."
>
> What is happening? Is this temporary? Or if a permanent transformation, is it unique? There is a pattern of "maturation" among males into which John Henry may fit. If so, he is about to "settle down," take on more familial responsibility, worry more, spend less time with the boys fishing, hunting, drinking, riding around. This kind of change usually occurs in age-range from 35-45. There are few "good old boys" over 40.

In the case of females, the peer group does not seem to play so important a role, though women do sometimes have gossip partners, and they can commiserate with other women. A certain group of ladies who commute to work together in a carpool may constitute a peer group similar to their male counterparts. In general, in families of Types III and IV from childhood on, the woman's place is in the home, while in families of Types I and II it may be either at home or at work. In either event, there is little room left for peer group loyalty or activity.

Theodore Newcomb, in connection with the famous Bennington College study, wrote: "In this community, as presumably in most others, all individuals belong to the total membership group, but such membership is not necessarily a point of reference for every form of social adaptation."[9] At Bennington, Newcomb found that although everyone belonged to the same larger group, they used different reference standards in shaping their attitudes and adaptations; although everyone in Shiloh would claim the community as a membership group, it does not serve as a single reference group for its citizens.

Since few direct questions were asked of informants concerning reference groups and standards, differences in reference phenomena must be inferred largely from other information, particularly the expressed values and attitudes toward certain figures and standards and knowledge of differences in exposure to figures who could become reference sources (e.g., differences in the Wilson's "scale").

Many reference figures are available to the people of Shiloh; a partial list would include peer groups, outmigrant kin and friends, other family members, persons in various

[9] Theodore Newcomb, "Attitude Development as a Function of Reference Groups: The Bennington Study," in *Readings in Social Psychology*, ed. E. E. Maccoby, T. M. Newcomb, and E. L. Hartley, 3d ed. (New York: Henry Holt, 1958), 274-75.

social levels and role models from the locale, county or regional businessmen, politicians and culture heroes, and groups and individuals from the outside both real and constructed from mass media and hearsay. It seems likely that changes have occurred in the influence which these different referents have had on normative standards, on aspirations, and on adaptive modes, especially given the increasing number of persons and groups present from the outside, increasing migration, and increasing distribution of mass media instruments and improved transportation and communication. For example, Mrs. Greene mentioned that she liked to read. "I read an awful lot of books in the winter." I asked her, "Do you think that reading and getting outside and watching television has influenced your way of life or your tastes?" She replied, "Oh, I know it has. Books have influenced me a lot."

Notes on an admittedly atypical Type IV man record that he also reads a great deal: "He says he would just as soon read as watch TV. . . . His fancy runs mostly to mysteries and Zane Grey. He likes men's magazines, too. His wife reads, too, mostly love stories, which Carl does not care for. 'I don't like to read about other people's troubles.' He has read enough things besides mysteries and westerns to be conversant about the Nuremburg trials, Indians ('There's about 500 different bands, according to the encyclopedia.'), author Howard Fast, and existing prison conditions and attempts at rehabilitation reforms." Likewise, a Type I man, somewhat the adventurer, "says he has always wanted to go to Alaska. A cousin now lives in Anchorage. When I mentioned Australia, he was full of facts about bushmen and snakes; he has seen something in the *National Geographic*."

As might be expected from the characteristics of family types already presented, there is a kind of continuum of referents running from local to outside which parallels the scale formed by the family types and the Wilsons' scale.

Types III and IV families seem most oriented toward local reference figures, and these figures are mostly on the same social level. The men appear to take their cues from their peers, and reject higher-status and outside standards. John Henry Sommers, for example, allowed that "some people try to live too high; sometimes they get above their raising. Sometimes they fall back down pretty quick, too. I just like a full belly and take one day at a time." Fundamentalist preachers played down the need for education and money. One man didn't like eating with "town folks," another didn't like "big churches," and another rejected the "new Bible" (Revised Standard Version) because he considered it to be Communist-linked.

The women in these families, on the other hand, are more prone to use higher-status local and outside reference figures. John Henry, for instance, after derogating people who "spread the mayonnaise pretty thick" and "get above their raising," admitted, "A lot of women, though, want things better and look into the future." Ernest Phelps thought it was generally true in Shiloh that "women usually want more things than men. The average man feels like a lot of things aren't needed that a woman wants." The outside may not be as important a referent for Type III and Type IV women as it is for women in other family types.

At the other end of the scale of family types, although influenced by kinfolk and other Type I families, the Type I's are much more oriented toward the outside, both real and imagined, as a source of reference figures. It is probable that outmigrants from their social level, friends and business contacts made from outside, symbolic referents constructed from newspaper society columns, books, movies, and other mass media, and emissaries from the outside (such as tourists) constitute the bulk of referents that influence the normative standards and comparisons of Type I family members. Craig Bowman reflected one day, for example, "I like it here, too, but sometimes I think about some of the boys I knew in college. Some of them weren't as smart as I was, and this one boy cleared $10,000 last year and may clear $25,000 this year." The Greenes, for another example, "plan to build a new home somewhere in the Shiloh area soon. They prefer the modern, ranch-type architecture. Most of the ideas they will use in building have come from house plans they have collected over the years from newspapers and magazines and from Mr. Greene's work as a contractor."

Type II families and Type III families range between the extremes on the local-outside dimension of reference figures. The Type II's tend to use outside reference figures as well as local ones. Many of the men, for example, mention their experiences in the service or the people they met, things they saw and did while employed somewhere outside the mountains. Locally, they are oriented toward middle and upper social level groups, but they are influenced by figures from lower social levels as well—for example, by former peer group members, church members, and relatives from lower on the social scale. A hypothesis worth testing is that Type II's use lower level reference figures for normative orientations but upper level groups for comparison types of reference.

Type III families tend to fall toward the more local, lower-status level in their reference figures. They are much more oriented toward peers, family members (including older generations, whom Types I and II sometime ignore), and same- and lower-level groups than are I's and II's but they are also sufficiently exposed to mass media and other outside influences to look in that direction, too. The women are particularly likely to use higher-level and outside referents.

Thus, there exists a considerable range of reference figures and standards in Shiloh, a wider range than Weller notes among West Virginia's mountain people in this passage: "The more limited the outlook of the persons involved, the more likely is the reference group to be confined to family members, and the less comfortable the person will be in outside contacts. The more upwardly mobile persons, those exhibiting more nearly middle class tendencies, will belong to one or more groups composed of like-minded friends, who will most often be close neighbors."[10] It is not only important to take note of the range of reference figures existing in the community, but also of the fact that in any particular family type there are likely to be several groups and figures used for normative and comparative reference.

Any source that is relied on for potential solutions to problems is considered an adaptive resource. One's self may constitute such a resource, as may a family, a peer group, or a subculture.[11] Since we have stated that a major problem operating in Shiloh is economic (how to make a living), one main area in which to differentiate among kinds of resources is economic. This has already been done in the case of employment, which has been used as a basic starting point in the construction of family types. But there are other kinds of resources besides economic, and there are other kinds of economic resources besides occupation. A more general list of resources might include, besides work, the individual's own problem-solving skills, members of the immediate family, the extended family, friends, neighbors, storekeepers, ministers and churches, doctors, employers, banks and finance companies, teachers

[10] Weller, *Yesterday's People,* 78. See also 79-81.

[11] Harvey Smith makes frequent use of the concept of adaptive resources. See Harvey L. Smith, "Society and Health in a Mountain Community," Working paper of the Social Research Section of the Division of Health Affairs and the Institute for Research in Social Science, University of North Carolina, Chapel Hill, 1963, p. 7. See also Marc Fried, "Effects of Social Change on Mental Health," *American Journal of Orthopsychiatry,* XXXIV (Jan. 1964), 3-28.

and schools, government agencies, mass media (which provide models for problem-solving—"Peyton Place" and "Dear Abby" play Dutch uncle to millions).

Except for the resource of personal skills, any of those mentioned can be classified somewhere along a primary-secondary continuum (or a personal-nonpersonal continuum).[12] The resources just listed are given more or less in order of decreasing primariness from the point of view of the residents of Shiloh. My observations in the field indicate that, with certain important exceptions, secondary resources are used to a greater extent by families toward the top of the scale of types, whereas primary resources are used by those toward the bottom. This is shown, for instance, in borrowing patterns, in Type I families' greater use of banking and legal resources, and in their greater willingness to buy and sell land to strangers for profit. Contrast the following two passages from the field notes, the first a quote from Craig Bowman, the second from James Haskell:

> I plan to build a road to my new property, lot it off, and sell it to summer people or people who want a place in the mountains for a week or so at a time.

> James said a Florida man tried to buy some land from him: "He says, 'How much would you take for just an acre?' I says, 'Well, mister, if you was to buy it, you'd know it. That piece you want is right in the middle of my field.' He says, 'How much you want for it?' I told him I'd take $2,000 for that one acre. He says, 'That's a little high for me.' I says, 'It's s'posed to be. I don't know you and you don't know me, and I'd

[12] Although the term *primary* is Charles H. Cooley's, the dimension here is more than a type of social relationship; it involves the basis on which the decision to use a resource is made. At one extreme is the person who asks, "Is it familiar?" while at the other is the person who asks, "Is it efficient?" This dimension is somewhat related to Gans's "person-orientation" and "object-orientation" (see Gans, *The Urban Villagers*, 89-97).

> have to know who you are and what you want and what you was going to use this land for before I'd think about selling you any of it.' "

Cyrus Johnson's study of 324 Kentucky mountain families receiving Aid to Dependent Children shows the different ways in which the unemployed heads of households (many of which would be Type IV's) seek work. He reports that "the method of seeking work most often indicated was that of asking friends and relatives," with application at public employment offices running second and use of private employment agencies and newspaper advertisements running last.[13] It would not be surprising to find the same pattern in Shiloh among comparable families.

Resource usage is therefore clearly related to values. In addition to variation in *usage* among the family types, there is also the matter of *availability,* which varies by family type, too.

Since literacy is less frequent in Type IV families, readership is less common; fewer forms are filled out and fewer letters are written. Those at the lower end of the scale of family types have little knowledge of banking and financing—and little collateral as well. On the other hand, those further up the scale know better how to search out people, agencies, books that will be the most efficient in helping solve a problem. Such knowledge and skill make certain resources available in a sense that they would not be otherwise. The government, the library, and the bank, like the hammer and saw, are useful instruments, but only if one knows how to wield them.

Convenience is another aspect of availability. Some resource persons, for example, are easier to reach than others, and hence they are more likely to be used. Ease of transportation and telephone communication are impor-

[13] Cyrus M. Johnson, "Mountain Families in Poverty" (unpublished paper, Departments of Sociology and Rural Sociology, University of Kentucky, Social Research Service and the Agricultural Experiment Station Cooperating, May 1965), 17-22.

tant factors in this connection. Certain resources may be specifically designed only for certain types of families—for example, welfare programs—and are therefore not available as resources to most families of Types I, II, and III.

With the latter exception, almost all the resources of the secondary type mentioned earlier are more closed to Type IV families than to any of the other types, and they become relatively less closed as one moves up the scale. The reverse appears to be the case with primary resources, but it is not as strong a tendency: even Type I families count on one another and friends for help and support at times, though they are usually merely supplementary to secondary sources. In the case of Type IV's, the family, friends, neighbors, storekeepers, ministers—all primary sources—are the major sources of help (we must add welfare for some) when problems arise.

III. *Family Structure*

Several difficulties attend the study of family structure, not the least of which is the absence of clear guidelines concerning what family structure is or what aspects of it should be studied. Paradoxically, it sometimes seems there are too many ways to go about describing structure. The choices of emphasis in this chapter are therefore to some extent arbitrary, and it is recognized that other aspects could have been chosen for description and analysis. The rule of thumb used has simply been to include those aspects of family structure which seem to show some significant patterned variation among the four family types, and which appear important for a discussion of familial adaptive problems and responses. Thus, the present discussion plays down the traditional anthropological type of comparisons of kinship structure and emphasizes such social structural variables as household composition, authority, task-allocation, nuclear-extended relations, and intergenerational relations.

A simple description of household composition and family size is a way of providing the basic brushstrokes in a picture of family structure. The household or domestic group is chosen as a unit of analysis because of its empirical convenience.

In terms of size, although no precise figures are available for comparison, it was clear from observation in the field that Type I families were the smallest and Type IV families the largest, with Types II and III ranging between. One Type IV family included nine children, the oldest around twelve years, with both parents still in their thirties.[1] The larger number of children can be accounted for by an incomplete understanding of birth control methods and by negative attitudes and even religious sanctions against the use of contraceptives. A social caseworker remarked about the family just mentioned: "They have nine children and the tenth one on the way. She is in very poor health and has been since the fourth one. The doctor told her after the fourth one she shouldn't have any more. She changed doctors. Their religion keeps them from believing in sterilization. [The family is fundamentalist.] If she could be told that she had to have a total operation [hysterectomy], she would do it, but she won't have her tubes tied. And she doesn't need a total operation."

Types III and IV families are also larger because of occasional extended kin living in. One household includes a man and his wife, their sons, one married daughter and her husband (when he is not off roaming the country), a grandchild who is the offspring of this last union, and, until recently, another married daughter and a grandmother. Hope Sommers once noted that she enjoyed living in Connecticut for a brief time because "people don't visit and drop in all the time and come to live with you like they do here." John Henry agreed, adding, "Why, you know, there's been somebody living with us ever since we got married. Not just all short visits, either." (His brother-in-law has lived with them for two years.)

At the level of Types III and IV families, one is also more likely to find a phenomenon that might be termed part-time residence, in which kin drop in for short or long periods of time. This term best describes the case just mentioned. The open-door policy of many Types III and IV families means that their household composition fluctuates with greater rapidity than those at other levels.

[1] By June 1966, a tenth child had been added.

It is often said that families are closer in the mountains than elsewhere, and informants in Shiloh certainly give verbal testimony to this. Craig Bowman's wife, Barbara, for example, remarked about mountain families, compared to ones she had known in a piedmont city, "I think they are much closer knit than families in the city. I can remember all Craig talked about before we got married was his family and how he loved it up here." In what sense this closeness is a fact, if it is a fact, is not clear, but the sentiment that underlies the statement is nonetheless significant. There is a feeling which runs throughout the community that families are important, as Kaplan has also noted.[2]

Kaplan reports that there is concern in some parts of Shiloh that families are no longer close. How long this has been a concern, and whether, indeed, families are not as cohesive today as in the past is not known, but it is apparent that many families are not close in at least a physical sense and that there are significant divergences of values and attitudes within families.

I would suggest that physical closeness and psychological closeness, which might be termed solidarity, can be distinguished from each other, and that they may not vary together. Families can be dispersed but feel solidarity; they can be centralized but lack solidarity. By and large it appears that kin solidarity, as an abstract, nonspecific value prescribing sentiments such as family loyalty and parental love and respect is widespread throughout the community, even though physical togetherness is not always found. The decline in visiting expressed by informants has already been noted. Migration has also removed family members for varying lengths of time. But the psychological ties have usually survived, as this excerpt

[2] Berton H. Kaplan, "Social Change, Adaptive Problems, and Health in a Mountain Community" (unpublished Ph.D. dissertation, University of North Carolina, 1962), Chap. 8.

from my field notes indicates: "When in the past he has traveled to other places to work, Clyde Harmon has always left his family behind. I asked him how it worked out to leave his family behind. He said it seemed to work out OK. I asked if he noticed any difference in the family when he returned. 'No, nothing I can think of except we was always glad to be back together, always happier. We never drifted apart, if that's what you mean. We was closer, if anything.'" Families may be dispersed; but they gather still for church homecomings and family reunions, as this note from early fall indicates: "The Labor Day weekend marks the end of one thing and the beginning of something else. Visits home by outmigrants are the heaviest since July 4th; 'It might be the last chance we get to come up for a while.' Spontaneous reunions clutter the community." Thus, family expressions of closeness in Shiloh did not seem to me to be affected by mere physical apartness.

Regarding extended family relations, Types I and II seem to have somewhat greater physical separation between households than Types III and IV. There appeared to be less daily contact among relatives of Types I and II (possibly because more of them were working than were family members on lower levels), and their households are frequently situated farther apart.[3] There are, however, exceptions to this tendency, such as the Bowmans, where four related Type I households are adjacent to one another. Likewise, there are Type IV families where the siblings are dispersed—the Howard Haskells are one example. The latter type are mostly drifters who have unstable household locations but who do visit family members frequently (eighteen people stayed overnight in Howard's house on July 4).

[3] The contrast between Rivers Cove, Yellowjacket, and lower Silver Creek on the one hand, and any section of the main highway on the other, is striking in this regard.

There does not seem to be so much variation in feelings of family solidarity from one type to another as there does in sheer physical closeness. The phenomena of kin migration do not provide exceptions to these generalizations concerning extended kin relations. If a person travels long distances, he comes home sooner; if he plans to stay outside a long time, he settles closer to home. Although visiting home is frequent at all levels, it is perhaps more frequent at the lower levels, holding constant such things as distance and car ownership.

It is difficult to generalize about variations in help patterns in extended families of different types, because the ability to help and the form of help may not be comparable. A member of a Type I family can help another member with such things as personal references, lending of money, and signatures on loans. A member of a Type IV family, on the other hand, has very little money and no influential business contacts. When he helps a kinsman it is with his time, his talents, however meager they may be, and his food, clothes, and home: he is willing to share whatever he has within wide limits, to the right person. Guy Patrick expressed this often-heard sentiment when he said, "We're just poor people and ain't got much, but you're welcome to say and eat with us and come back any time." When I enjoyed Howard Haskell's hospitality one suppertime, he announced, as we walked in the house, "Now, we ain't got any plumbing in the house, and the pump's busted now, but here's you some clean water, and there's the soap and a towel. And here's the comb. You can comb here in the living room if you want, where there's a glass."

It seems to be the case that, even though their resources are more limited, families of Types III and IV are more willing to extend the help pattern beyond the limit of the circle of households formed by parents and their offspring, typically fenced off for aid purposes in Types I and II families. Thus, Royce Rogers, a Type II who was asked whether he helped or received help from any of the many other shrubbery-haulers when downcountry, replied that they helped each other out sometimes, but not too often. His brother Cleveland confided later that he and Royce and the two other Rogers brothers in the shrubbery business rarely helped each other. The help circle among III's and IV's, on the other hand, may more typically widen out to embrace some uncles, cousins, in-laws, and neighbors. John Henry Sommers' haircutting service is a good example of this. He cuts hair, free, for every man and boy who drops by the house and asks him—brothers, uncles, neighbors, friends, and even a sociologist. He himself has his hair cut at the barbershop for a dollar and a half. One man has even taken in four children and raised them, boys who were thrown out or abandoned by their parents: two brothers from nearby, one Indian boy, and an "ex-convict."

In explaining the pattern of greater nuclearization among higher level families, some conclusions drawn by Eric R. Wolf in his study of peasant life are applicable:

> The prevalence of wage-labor is [one] condition for the emergence of the nuclear family. As soon as peasants turn into wage-laborers the likelihood that nuclear families will prevail increases vastly, especially where the labor contract involves a single-interest exchange of wages for labor performed, without any additional relations between employer and worker, [where people] are employed for their individual labor-power, not for that of their entire families.
>
> . . . We may say that we are likely to find nuclear families where the division of labor is accentuated in society, but not in the family, while extended families are consistent with an accentuated division of labor within the family, but not in society.

Division of labor is, of course, heavily stepped up with the growth of industrialism. Industrialism has

> an almost immediate effect on the number of people in agriculture. As jobs in industry become available those underemployed or only seasonally employed in agriculture emigrate to seek factory jobs.[4]

Wolf defines peasants as "rural cultivators," differentiating them from agricultural entrepreneurs. "The peasant does not operate an enterprise in the economic sense; he runs a household, not a business concern."[5] In Wolf's terms, the differences in nuclear-extended family relations in Shiloh can be partly accounted for by the increasing movement of families away from peasanthood and toward industrialization.

Every student of the Southern mountains from Kephart to Weller has come away with a definite picture of strict patriarchal authority in the home.[6] There are many examples of this particular distribution of authority in Shiloh today, but there are also some significant departures from this form which deserve attention.

One form is the matriarchal family. Many of the matriarchies in Shiloh would also be classified as matrifocal families, since the mother exercises her power in the absence of her husband, who has deserted or died.[7] Though not numerous, this is an important subtype. Part

[4] Eric R. Wolf, *Peasants* (Englewood Cliffs, N.J.: Prentice-Hall, 1966), 70-72.

[5] *Ibid.*, 2.

[6] Horace Kephart, *Our Southern Highlanders,* 2d ed. (New York: Macmillan, 1922), 330 ff.; Jack E. Weller, *Yesterday's People* (Lexington: University of Kentucky Press, 1965), Chap. 4; Marion Pearsall, *Little Smoky Ridge: The Natural History of a Southern Appalachian Neighborhood* (University: University of Alabama Press, 1959), 98 ff.; Alberta Pierson Hannum, "The Mountain People," in *The Great Smokies and the Blue Ridge,* ed. Roderick Peattie (New York: Vanguard, 1943), 125-28.

[7] See Raymond T. Smith, *The Negro Family in British Guiana* (London: Routledge and Kegan Paul, 1956). Also Lee D. Kittredge, "The Matrifocal Family and Mental Health" (unpublished paper, University of North Carolina).

of the significance of matrifocal families is that their existence gives testimony to the ability of women in the community to wield authority effectively without benefit of male leadership. There are in Shiloh several outstanding examples of matrifocal families in which offspring and even grandchildren have been cared for, educated, and started up the ladders of success which their matriarchs have set before them. One widowed grandmother, Mrs. Simpson, takes pride in having cared for her divorced daughter and her two children, one of whom has finished business college and the other of whom has her first job on the outside at the age of twenty. The existence of such families also indicates that many women in the community place great value on success and are also in other ways oriented toward the ways of the outside world. Four of the six matriarchal-matrifocal families I was able to list are very much caught up in the mainstream of American society.

The existence of a familial authority pattern such as this seems to demonstrate that beneath the solid, unwavering patriarchal front of many mountain families there lies submerged and unacknowledged great female power. It is like an undercurrent which cannot be seen but which nevertheless helps shape shorelines and surface movement. Men like Howard Haskell, Clyde Harmon, and John Henry Sommers may publicly proclaim their sovereignty, but women, even in the most patriarchal of households, are not without power to influence their men and children. Though in public they often seem servile (they have learned the art of being obedient at strategic times), obedience is not to be confused with powerlessness. Aunt Polly Bodkin, a venerable great-grandmother, assumes such power over her family, now scattered into their households in the community, that "she tells fifty-year-old grandfathers how to run their houses." Yet, she says of the time when her husband was alive, "My old man used to be the boss; he wore the britches. I always did whatever he said. He was sick and invalid for a long time, too, and I still done just what he said." Another lady once said, "I believe the man should be the head. A woman, you know, can get her way kind of subtly." Later she said, "Any man likes to *feel* he's the head. You learn when to go along." Thus, the husband sometimes has "ceremonial" functions but not real economic or managerial power. In less extreme cases, the wife has influence, if not control.

There is another important family authority pattern in Shiloh different from both the paper-tiger patriarchy and the matriarchal-matrifocal types: the equalitarian type, more frequent among Types I and II families. Many informants, male and female, acknowledge that the position of women is changing and that more families are becoming equalitarian. Aunt Polly, for example, after describing her loyal subordination, added, "Women ain't like that no more." Ollis Vance said, "You take even ten years ago I bet there wasn't but one or two [women] worked. And like we were talking about, some women—well, it's like this old saying, some men are under the women's petticoats." Craig Bowman noted that an increasing number of wives were keeping separate accounts at the store because they didn't want to have to depend on their husbands to pay for "little personal things that their wives buy—like clothes and shoes." Most of these are workingwomen. Flora Cline observed that "nowadays, when a woman works, she can go off on her own. There used to be only a few women worked and we didn't have that."

Census figures reporting an increasing percentage of the labor force to be women make the argument plausible that having access to economic power has advanced women's positions in the home. Whatever the trend from the past, there are now a number of families in Shiloh, mainly Types I and II, which approach the equalitarian form: both men and women work outside the home, major decisions are not made without advice and consent from both spouses, and, frequently, household management tasks are divided between husband and wife and not automatically relegated to a subordinated wife-mother. Thus, one wife is able to report, "We spend our own money. What he wants to buy, he buys. What he wants to sell, he sells. The same with me. He has his furniture, I have mine."

This distribution of authority bothered many residents. Not many women expressed this feeling, but Aunt Polly made a statement that many of the *men* would have endorsed: "Why, anybody knows, the way things are going, the women and the colored is taking over. Might as well just put them in the same boat." Howard Haskell was disturbed about the trend, and John Henry said that if he were married to one particular bossy woman, he'd "put a stop to that in a hurry!" But most of the families that could be called equalitarian were not especially disturbed about the distribution of authority in their own homes, and they felt it worked very well. One man reports that his wife "likes working, herself. She'd rather be home with the family, but she likes work all right. No, I don't think she's asked for any more say in how the money's spent or anything since she's been working. It all goes in the same pot, just like before she went to work." Thelma Flood, in an unusual, equalitarian Type III family, said:

> One thing about Roy and me, he never tells me what to do and I don't tell him what to do. We just kindly make up our own minds about what we want to do. Sometimes I'll want his opinion on something, want to know what he thinks about it, but he won't even say then. He'll say whatever I think will be all right. It was that way about me working.
>
> I think he is less bossy [than most men]. And he

> don't mind my working. I asked him if he thought it would be all right for me to buy the groceries and he could take care of the rest and he said that would be all right, so now I buy all the groceries and he pays the other bills. Then he gives me money when he has any extra, just like if I wasn't working.

Unlike the seemingly threatened advocates of patriarchy, few of the men expressed feelings that tradition was being destroyed or that the Bible was being overthrown. In short, as might be expected, the Types I and II who had equalitarian families were mostly those who would consider themselves modern and who would tend to orient themselves to outside standards.

The present discussion has concentrated on variations in positions of men and women in authority structures. Typical families also include children and extended kin. Children in Shiloh are universally subject to the authority of their parents, as they are in most families elsewhere. It appears, however, that there are differences in the degree to which parents extend that authority. Type I's appear to be more strict, exercise more surveillance, and control the hourly and daily behavior of their children more than do Type IV's. Ernest Phelps watches his children closely and makes conscious attempts to train them in habits of diligence, cleanliness, and foresight. Howard Haskell wouldn't know where to find his children even if he did want to discipline them; they run free except for sporadic disciplining. Clyde Harmon is about halfway between these two, espousing stern discipline and virtuous life habits, but seldom doing anything to bring them about.

Male children of Type IV's generally achieve independence at a relatively early age, and their parents do not seem to exercise control at all from the teen years on. The other two family types fall between the extremes of Types I and IV in this regard. This pattern does not mean that children in Type IV families have more authority over the rest of the family than children in other types of families; it merely means that they have more control over their own affairs. (Authority is essentially "relative power exercised by an individual over another."[8])

If there are other persons living in the family, their status is generally below that of the head of the household; older people seem to take a backseat in most family affairs. Other extended kin living in the household share many of the rights of conjugal members, but, like older persons, their authority is not great. In all cases of authority relations, naked exercise of power is seldom seen, and being bossy is taboo. Preserving smooth, friendly relationships is very important throughout the community, just as Gulick describes the "harmony ethic" among the "conservative" Cherokee Indian.[9]

Every family has some more or less institutionalized system of accomplishing its tasks and organizing its activities. Though not always agreed upon, the norms specifying who is to do what are usually fairly well understood.

One way to study family structure is to observe typical rounds of family activity and task accomplishment and thereby to chart the assignments of various members. Since the specific tasks vary among types, it is difficult to differentiate them in a way that is both concrete and comparable. It seems more advantageous, therefore, to categorize general types of task along comparable dimensions rather than to relate who plants the tobacco and who carries out the garbage. There are several sources in the literature to which one might turn for family task or activity schemes.

[8] Mirra Komarovsky, *The Unemployed Man and His Family* (New York: Dryden Press, 1940), 9.

[9] John Gulick, *Cherokees at the Crossroads* (Chapel Hill: Institute for Research in Social Science, 1960).

In terms of Talcott Parsons' scheme, the Type I and Type II families in Shiloh, with some exceptions, tend to be like those of the rest of the American middle class: approaching "equal allocation."[10] Frequently the earning of a living is shared between husband and wife, as is child rearing and discipline, buying, and major decision-making. Frequently there is no clear pattern, as in the case of a Type III man, Ollis Vance, who, because his wife works, admits, "I have to do some of the cooking. But the girls are a help with that. Then I have to do the gardening, too." John Henry, for another example, sometimes helps with the babysitting while Hope works.

Certain other families in the community, many of them among the Types III and IV, are more like what Parsons describes as typical: the father is the primary executive member, and the mother is the warm, indulgent conciliator. But there are many exceptions to this pattern. Indeed, upon closer inspection the more typical family of Type III or Type IV seems to demonstrate a confusion of instrumental and expressive roles. Among III's and IV's there are many instances where the wife has a definite economic function (galacking, factory job, store clerking, cafe counterwoman), though it does not seem to be as central to her life as a job is to Types I and II women.[11] The reason one woman went to work, for example, is because, "I didn't have no kids and it wasn't anything to do at the house but set around all day." Frequently the women rather than the men deal with representatives of the welfare agency, perhaps because the men are gone from the home most of the time leaving the women in charge. It is often the women who are more concerned with the training of children: it is Hope and not John

[10] Talcott Parsons and Robert F. Bales, *Family Socialization and Interaction Process* (Glencoe, Ill.: Free Press, 1955), 47, 317-18, and Chap. 7.

[11] Hope's case is a good example; she would take a job and quit every few weeks or months, depending on whether she could get a babysitter, whether she missed being with her family, etc.

Henry, for instance, who pushes education for her children and provides piano lessons for two of them. Often it is the mother who is less indulgent when it comes to discipline. Thus, while it is true that the father is given titular executive rights, the mother takes over a number of instrumental duties from the father, who plays a mixture of instrumental and expressive roles.

In the Type II family the father plays the more typical (to Parsons) instrumental role. In some Type II and many Type I families, this instrumental role is more frankly shared with the mother, as in the Parsonian American middle-class nuclear family.

Application of the Parsonian scheme of task allocation to families of Shiloh may be summarized by saying that:

1. Parsons' observation of instrumental-expressive role differentiation in which the male is assigned the former functions and the female the latter applies to some Shiloh families, but by no means to the majority;

2. the majority of families of Type I, and some of Type II, tend to follow the equal allocation model described by Parsons as typical of middle-class America;

3. the families of Types III and IV, and some of Type II, perhaps come as close as any to showing the usual functional differentiation, but mothers here often play a subdued instrumental role and fathers often play expressive roles.

Somewhat similar conclusions are reached when the scheme Elizabeth Bott used to classify British families is applied. Since her classification involves a different emphasis on differentiation, it may provide some additional insights into Shiloh families. Her classification is described as follows:

> In *complementary organization* the activities of husband and wife are different and separate but fitted together to form a whole. In *independent organization* activities are carried out separately by husband

> and wife without reference to each other, insofar as this is possible. In *joint organization* activities are carried out by husband and wife together, or the same activity is carried out by either partner at different times. . . .
>
> The phrase *segregated conjugal role-relationship* is here used for a relationship in which complementary and independent types of organization predominate. . . . The phrase *joint conjugal role-relationship* is here used for a relationship in which joint organization is relatively predominant.[12]

Bott found that the type of relationship varied most with the form of relationships external to the family: the degree to which social networks external to the family (such as peer groups and kin groups) were connected or the degree to which persons in a family member's network knew and met each other. The more connected the social network, the greater the likelihood of segregation of conjugal roles. She also observed that the segregated type of conjugal relationship was likely to be found on the working class level, and cites literature with similar findings.[13]

The findings for Shiloh families are in many ways comparable to those of Bott in Britain. It appears that in Types I and II families, joint organization is most typical. Complementary organization of conjugal role-relationships predominates in many families. Independent organization predominates in families of Types III and IV. Thus, there is greater segregation of conjugal role-relationships toward the lower end of the scale of family types, while joint relationships are more typical near the top, an observation consistent with the Parsonian interpretation. This pattern is clearest in the case of recreational and social activities. Except for visiting, families of Types III and IV seldom

[12] Elizabeth Bott, *Family and Social Network* (London: Tavistock, 1957), 53.

[13] *Ibid.*, 58 ff., 64 ff.

do things together (some do attend church together); typically, the husband is off hunting or fishing or loafing while the wife stays at home. Type I families, at the other extreme of the scale, stay at home together, vacation together, and attend social gatherings together.

Bott's findings regarding tightness of social networks is also consistent with our observations. The greater the orientation toward a peer group, a phenomenon more prevalent among III's and IV's, the greater the likelihood of segregated conjugal relationships. Weller has also noted this parallel between Bott's British families and West Virginia mountain families.[14]

One possible interpretation of these findings is that when networks are loose-knit, the couple is thrown together, and the family serves the function of emotional support. One makes his strongest emotional investment where there is the most continuity or stability. It may also be that "close-knit networks . . . interfere with conjugal solidarity."[15] Bott concludes that there are a number of personality, familial, occupational, and other factors interacting in a complex way to result in the discovered pattern. We can conclude no less regarding Shiloh.

Children are generally given few task assignments except in Type I and some Type II families. Girls are given more chores than boys, the former being called on for housekeeping, babysitting, and errand-running. The boys in Types III and IV (and some Type II) families are left relatively free to "loaf around the village store," as a minister observed even in the first decade of this century,[16] but girls and Type I boys are not so fortunate.

Elderly persons, especially women, appear to serve

[14] Weller, *Yesterday's People,* 73-76.

[15] Bott, *Family and Social Network,* 94.

[16] Edgar Tufts, *The Women of the Mountains* (pamphlet published by the Executive Committee of Home Missions of the Presbyterian Church in the United States, ca. 1910).

certain functions in families toward the bottom of the scale of types, where they are more likely to be found living with younger relatives. It is possible that older persons live with these families more frequently because such families cannot so easily afford separate housing, but also because there does not seem to be as much difference in values and outlooks between the generations. Their duty assignments are usually in household management, gardening, babysitting, and the like. Elderly men sometimes offer patriarchal advice, but they are customarily passive observers of the family scene. This seems to be the case in all family types, but the number of families with elderly persons living in them is so small that any generalizations must be very tentative.

The variations in task-allocation to men and women reflect some of the differences in the distribution of authority. This is especially noteworthy in the case of the woman, whose increased legitimated authority in families at the top of the scale (as opposed to her underground power, more typical toward the bottom) occurs concomitantly with her increased aboveboard instrumental functions (mainly economic).

If it can be assumed, as it is here, that there is a general upward trend among families in Shiloh with regard to the scale of types—that is, that there is a general upgrading as indicated by the relative proportion of families in each type over a period of time—then the differences in patterns of authority and task-allocation take on significance beyond mere ethnological reporting. Variations in family patterns like these indicate a potential source of adaptive problems to many husbands, wives, children, elderly persons, and other kin.

"Behold thou are old, and thy sons walk not in thy ways" (1 Sam. 8:5). It would be tempting but inappropriate to make a blanket statement concerning the existence in Shiloh of the sentiment expressed in this quotation. This sentiment, like most of the characteristics discussed in these pages, exists in different forms and intensities at various levels of community life.

If the general category of intergenerational relations is narrowed to only the area of values and attitudes—i.e., whether generations share or do not share the same values—the discussion is still complicated by the fact that specific values must be singled out. One value may be shared, another may not. Furthermore, the kind of value shared or not shared may vary from one family type to another. On the other hand, residents of Shiloh do find it meaningful to speak of two basic value clusters: "old-timey ways" and "outside ways." This local usage makes it possible to describe differences in generational continuity and discontinuity among family types relatively simply.

The task may further be simplified if the present grandparents are referred to as the first generation, parents as the second, and grandchildren as the third. This gives an approximate idea of age groupings and is a little more precise than the usual dichotomy between older and younger generations.

In Shiloh it appears that families of Type I and Type IV display the greatest generational continuity, a fairly consistent holding of outlooks across all three generations. In the case of Type I's it is an outside outlook; in the Type IV families it is the traditional outlook. There are not enough data to allow the pinpointing of breaks in continuity among families of Types II and III, but the strong impression from firsthand observation of family interaction and from hearing comments made about family members is that there is more discontinuity among these families. In Type II families the break seems to occur between the first and second generations, while in Type III families the break seems to occur between the second and third generations.

It is possible that these attitudinal discontinuities are related to shifts upward in social level and family type on the part of second and third generations. This statement is more hypothesis than finding, however.

The continuity in Type IV families was noted by Craig Bowman when he remarked: "There is an interesting thing around here. There are some people who take on their parents' ways and even their beliefs—even though they have been to school and learned differently." His examples were Type IV families. Similarly, the continuity from Craig's father, Sam, to himself, and to what Craig projects for his children (such as college education) exemplifies the continuity in most Type I families.

Craig also commented that he thought the breaks in continuity among generations occurred at different points in different families.

> He noted that there were varying amounts of conflict among different sets of generations. The generation of his grandparents (70-85 years of age) has not changed at all, he says, but the generation of his parents (50's) has changed considerably. He says he is more like his father than his father is like *his* father.
>
> He also noted that in different social strata change took place in different generations. In the upper levels the generation of his father underwent change. In the middle and some of the lower levels change is taking place in his generation. And in much of the lower level, change is yet to occur. By change, he specifically mentioned attitudes toward work and making money, and religious attitudes.

The difference between those who have changed and those who have not, according to this informant, is marked by occupation and dress, among other things:

> Now you can draw a distinguishing line up here in the kinds of work people do. A lot of people here

> work in industry. . . . These industrial workers show what Madison Avenue would call "advancement." The women wear shorts, and they are more forthright in what they think. The other people work in timber, jigs and so forth. These women will have more old-fashioned ways. The way the men dress will be different, too. Overalls and workshoes are a sign of outdoor work; the men in industrial jobs will tend to wear slacks and slippers (dress shoes).

This perceptive informant reflects the intergenerational division that slices irregularly through Shiloh families. Again, it is not a simple alignment of youth against age, but an alignment of new against old wherever they face each other. In some families it is youth that embodies the new and stands against the old as represented by the parental generation; in others it is parents who stand against *their* parents; in still others all generations stand together.

There is clearly a fundamental bifurcation of the community into two cultural worlds. The values espoused and the normative standards encompassed by the old and new ways of life need to be described and illustrated in detail before the various aspects of structure and the other elements of the constructed typology of families become clear. Differential value orientations must also be understood before one can knowledgeably discuss kinds of adaptive problems faced by different families and the ways families respond to those problems.

IV. *The Two Worlds of Shiloh*

If it can be said that there is choice in our lives, then values are what guide our choices. Values can be specific or general, and perhaps the most general are the values that guide our choice of other values. As Kluckhohn and Strodtbeck note, "There would be no ordered, no systematic, value system without a directive tendency which both aids in the selection among possible value systems and also serves to give continuity to the total system."[1] These general values are themes that run through a series of more specific value-choices made by individuals and groups, and they may be inferred from the latter as well as being communicated directly in statements.[2]

Two polar types of general value themes or subcultures exist in Shiloh; their expression is noted in more specific areas such as work, education, family, and religion. The subject is of great importance since it is partly in terms of values that people interpret and respond to their settings, and since situations of great stress can be created when an individual's values are in conflict. In addition, values are not only learned by individuals, they are characteristic of cultures as well, so that through values the individual or his family can be linked with the larger unit of culture. Thus, what have been called general value themes may be considered in many respects separate cultures to which people orient themselves: subcultures, as that term is usually used.

It is an open question whether this set of differential values and norms constitutes a contraculture rather than a subculture. *Contraculture* is the term suggested by

Yinger for use "wherever the normative system of a group contains, as a primary element, a theme of conflict with the values of the total society, where personality variables are directly involved in the development and maintenance of the group's values, and wherever its norms can be understood only by reference to the relationships of the group to a surrounding dominant culture."[3] Such phenomena as delinquent, adolescent, class, ethnic, and occupational "subcultures" are often misnamed, according to Yinger, because they often have strong elements of conflict with a dominant culture. For example, differences in social class are not always simply subcultural variations. "They are in part responses to a frustrating situation. They are efforts to deal with the disjunction of means and ends."[4] To the extend that this is the case, "When the disjunction is reduced, the variations in value and behavior are reduced."[5]

Much current thinking would have it that one of the subcultures with which I am dealing here is *only* contraculture, and that it is a way of life which has developed to handle an environment of poverty, deprivation, and constant frustration.[6] This answer is too simple; rather, it is, as Yinger would suggest, a mixture of subculture and contraculture, for there are strong elements of tradition running through this subculture, elements on which more immediate, situational cultural responses to frustration have been built.

[1] Florence R. Kluckhohn and Fred L. Strodtbeck, *Variations in Value Orientations* (Evanston, Ill.: Row, Peterson, 1961), 8.

[2] See Herbert J. Gans's use of "focal concerns" in his book *The Urban Villagers* (Glencoe, Ill.: Free Press, 1962), 244 ff.

[3] J. Milton Yinger, "Contraculture and Subculture," *American Sociological Review*, XXV (Oct. 1960), 629.

[4] *Ibid.*, 634.

[5] *Ibid.*

[6] For example, Hughes describes one of the areas of Stirling County in these words: "Here is the face of a rejected community, built on pride of exactly the opposite values of the surrounding communities." Charles C. Hughes and others, *People of Cove and Woodlot* (New York: Basic Books, 1960), 245.

This discussion will take on more meaning if some of the main value-themes that differentiate the two subcultures of Shiloh are described. Although it is accurate to speak of two subcultures, this manner of speaking does not imply that there are two and only two groupings in the community, each of which espouses or is the carrier of one of these sets of values. Every person and every family carries both subcultures in some mixture; only the emphasis varies. Similarly, although it is possible to isolate certain value-themes analytically as if they were distinct species, empirically they are not so pure and distinct from each other.

In what might be called the traditional subculture are found such characteristics as shortened-time perspectives, value of self and family above larger collectivities, an atmosphere of contentment (or resignation, depending on which bias one chooses), or willingness to "do without," limited value of planning and management skills, a greater premium placed on the personal and familiar than the efficient or rational, and a sharp split between the worlds of men and women. Some of these are qualities noted by various researchers as belonging generally to the lower class.[7] Most of these characteristics have been attributed to the population of Appalachia in a somewhat blanket fashion by Weller, who, like many students of mountain people, is not always careful to draw attention to the highly significant departures from traditional ways of life within communities.[8] What I have found in Shiloh, and suspect holds for similar areas elsewhere, is that certain parts of the community participate in this subculture more than do others, and that in fact the traditional way is at many points engaged in a competitive struggle with a newer and quite different way of life.

[7] See Gans, *The Urban Villagers,* Chap. 11, for a review of pertinent studies.

[8] Jack E. Weller, *Yesterday's People* (Lexington: University of Kentucky Press, 1965).

The present description of the traditional subculture is drawn from my firsthand observations and from observations of others who have studied the contemporary mountain scene. It is also drawn from reports of past mountain life by social scientists, historians, and other students of Appalachia of the past. It is partly by right of this check on the past that this subculture is called the traditional.

Time perspective is one of the elements of the traditional subculture. Actually, it is not the length but the direction of the perspective which sets the traditional subculture off from middle-class America. The adequately socialized middle-class individual lives in the future: he plans ahead, he anticipates and enjoys future states in his imagination, he is taught to defer the gratifications of the moment for supposed greater reward in the ever-germinating but never-blooming long run. He stumbles through the present because his eyes are on the images of success, accomplishment, advancement, and career. To this man history is boring and without special utility or meaning, and the present is merely something to bear.

On the other hand, anthropologists have written of peoples such as the prerevolutionary Chinese whose roots are in the past, and whose orientation to the present is through the eyes of their ancestors. Riesman has also described a type, the tradition-directed man, whose guide-rules come from history and whose directions into the future are set by the past.

The traditional subcultural outlook in Shiloh takes its cues from the past to a certain extent, but the past culture itself seems to have been pretty much oriented to its present, so that the predominating quality of the present subculture is one of present-orientation.[9] John Henry Sommers expresses this present-orientation when he says,

[9] An article by Marion Pearsall describes similar impressions of time-perspective among traditional Southern Appalachian residents: "Communicating with the Educationally Deprived," *Mountain Life and Work* (Spring 1966), 8-11.

"I just like a full belly and take one day at a time." There is no slavish attempt to live the present exactly as the past was lived, except perhaps in the area of religion ("Give Me That Old-Time Religion" is still a favorite gospel song in the fundamentalist churches). Rather, most persons for whom this traditional outlook is characteristic tend to live in the present, with only occasional backward glances to the past and forward looks to the future.

Of course, living in the present is a relative matter, and no one can do it in an absolute sense. But one can live from day to day, week to week, month to month, or year to year without planning ahead for his needs and those of his family. Howard Haskell used to work at a mica jig that gradually was phased out of existence. He was the last to be phased, while his brother James (who, unlike Howard, still has a relatively steady job) was among the first to leave it for other work. Howard hung onto the old and familiar and refused to look to the future as his brother did. Carl Patrick preferred not to plant a garden last year because the lady on whose land he was squatting might have decided to clear the land and build on it. "I'd get paid for it all right," he said, "but I'd of hated to see it tore up." He must now borrow, beg, or buy his food.

Time, as measured by watches and clocks, is usually unimportant. Many homes do not have clocks; John Henry and Hope happened to have a built-in clock on the stove, though it didn't always work.[10] The natural rhythm of the seasons and daily cycles still sets the pace for much activity.

Planning for the future, if done at all, is sporadic. John Henry once said of me in a conversation with a third

[10] Pearsall also notes this aspect of the nebulosity of the future in her *Little Smoky Ridge: The Natural History of a Southern Appalachian Neighborhood* (University: University of Alabama Press, 1959), 81. See also Vladimir Hartman, "A Cultural Study of a Mountain Community" (unpublished Ph.D. dissertation, University of North Carolina, 1957).

party, "He looks ahead at things, which is good. That's something I don't ever do, but it's good." Getting running water in the house was a project that took several years: "John Henry is planning to put water in his house in a couple of weeks, when his uncle arrives for his vacation here. He also plans to get some help building cabinets, as his uncle is a carpenter of sorts. [Neither plan worked out, but the water and cabinets were installed during the following winter.] John Henry once dug a ditch for putting water in the house, but there is no trace of a ditch in the yard now—he never got around to laying the pipe." Planning and working for the future apply only to absolute necessities. As Clarence Haskell says, a man has to work "enough to keep the bill collectors away."

Perhaps this kind of foreshortened perspective reflects an adjustment to a multitude of life contingencies over which there is little felt control, whether they be occupational and economic, educational and natural, or political and legal. But although truncated time perspectives may have this functional consequence, it would be a mistake to declare them simply responses to lack of fate control, as we do not have the time-sequence data necessary to justify such an inference. It seems likely, furthermore, that this is an element of an older cultural heritage transmitted selectively to certain segments of this contemporary mountain community. We might tentatively conclude that this aspect of the traditional subculture—perhaps the whole of this subculture—is a synthesis of cultural heritage and response to social situation, and that to some extent people pick and choose from the cultures of their forebears in the light of contemporary needs.

An aspect of traditional subculture related to time perspective is the value placed on contentment. Ollis Vance gave expression to this value when he said, "We don't worry too much about things. I like to think of what old Uncle Joe said about they wasn't any use to worrying about things because life's too short for that. If he ever had a worry, you'd never know it; he was always whistling or talking to you about things. I think he had the right idea." Vergil Phelps told of a man with a similar outlook:

> There's some people around here that never did want nothing and don't want nothing now. They don't work steady, and they just make it from one day to the next.
>
> This one man, some feller from Tennessee come through here wanting him to get some training in TV repair. He's the best repairman and car mechanic you ever did see. But he won't work steady, just takes his time and works when he wants to. He told this feller he wouldn't go; said he'd lived all his life a poor man and he'd got kinda used to it. He's the happiest man you ever seen; not a worry in this world. Never saw him mad, either.

Kephart once referred to this as the land of "do without," noting that highlanders in the early part of the century had "a shrewd regard for essentials" and excluded "whatever can be done without."[11] One lady in Shiloh offers an example of this willingness to do without when she tells of a former neighbor Edgar McCall.

> Now, when Edgar was living over here in my brother's house, there for about three years I gave them quilts and curtains and I don't know how much canned goods and things. Then one day I was walking back from working in the garden. I was so hot my glasses were steaming, and I had to stop in front of Edgar's, and he was lying on the porch with his head on a sack of fertilizer in the cool. He said something about

[11] Horace Kephart, *Our Southern Highlanders*, 2d ed. (New York: Macmillan, 1922), 278.

> being so hungry that if the car in his yard was a big cake he could eat the whole thing. And then he said, "But I wouldn't work for it."

As with work, so with education. People who have dropped out of school say they regret it and will send their children through high school, but their sorrow and their intentions sound only half-sincere. Thus, Henry Haskell joked about being twenty-one when he finished the first grade, and he told a story about a man who, when asked how far he went in school, replied, "About two mile." John Henry says he will "try ever way I can" to get his children to finish high school, which is at best a qualified hope when contrasted with the automatic assumption of a college education for Craig Bowman's children.

The willingness to do without is usually interpreted by students of mountain life as the absence of goals and aspirations.[12] Indeed, there is no special emphasis on becoming somebody or attaining the marks of success which we believe men of worth are naturally born to covet. But the phrase "doing without" states a positive value negatively. If this is the way life in this subculture appears at first glance, it would be wrong to conclude that it is only a negation of middle-class aspirations or a sour-grapes attitude that finds its counterpart in the small boy who, when his cohorts refuse to let him play baseball with them, simply retreats, muttering between sniffles that he doesn't want to play ball anyway. That is, it is conceivable that some people do not now and never did want to play ball, but rather find their attentions caught by other kinds of activity which to us seem not worthwhile or entertaining. If one is willing to grant that goals other

[12] For example, see Claudia Lewis, *Children of the Cumberland* (New York: Columbia University Press, 1946), in which she contrasts children's personalities and family situations in Greenwich Village and a mountain settlement in eastern Tennessee.

than monetary success, the accumulation of status material, the exercise of power and privilege, and the never-ending climb to the top punctuated by periodic feelings of accomplishment are possible as legitimate ends in life, then he must also realize that the means to such goals may also lack particular value in some frames of reference. Where the major goals of life are the leisurely pursuit of nature (in the form of hunting and fishing), the maintenance of comradeship with one's friends and of one's position within a relatively small group of like-minded associates, the search for the security of salvation in another world, and the keeping of obligations to family, neighbor, and friend, there is no real need for formal education, for constant striving and straining, for self-advancement and self-betterment. These are means to an alien way of life.[13]

One of the key dimensions of the traditional outlook concerns the meaning of human relationships. In this subculture, kinship (sometimes referred to as familism)[14] and friendship are among the most important things in life. Even when people are disliked, they are disliked with a certain quality of depth and intimacy that may appear to the outside observer as unduly intense. People are judged in personal terms, on the basis of who they are, how they act toward other people, and what their pasts have been. This outlook extends to work and commercial relationships. Cal Underwood is one of several men who have worked in New Hampshire for a time; he liked the job because he liked the man he worked for, an understanding man. Cal said, "Course, I'd come home a lot. Ever once in a while I'd find me somebody to take my

13 "Bayard Rustin, the civil rights leader, tells the fearful story of trying to interest restless young Negroes in work and discovering that many of them preferred the life of the streets, stealing, or selling 'pot' (marijuana), or even pimping." Robert L. Heilbroner, "No Room at the Bottom," *Saturday Review* (Feb. 19, 1966), 32. See also Gans, *The Urban Villagers,* 251: "When opportunity factors are increasingly available, people respond by more fully implementing their subcultural aspirations."

14 Pearsall, *Little Smoky Ridge,* Chap. 6.

place on the hoist, and I'd got to the boss—he was from Riverview—and he'd let me off a couple of days to come home. He was good about that. It means a lot to work for somebody that understands you want to go home sometimes. He was from here and *knowed.*" Relationships to storekeepers, as well as to employers, are more appreciated if they have a strong personal element. One evening the writer overheard John Henry and Henry Haskell talking about storekeepers around Shiloh and their respective merits. I gathered that what is required to make a storekeeper popular is that he be friendly, helpful, and willing to extend credit occasionally. I recall that one of the stories John Henry told about being in Kentucky was about a storekeeper who was extraordinarily trusting and helpful in a particular emergency. He was close to being the Ideal Storekeeper. This desire for a strong personal element puts the storekeepers in a bind as they try increasingly to put their dealings on a purely business basis and get away from the image of the old-fashioned country store.

It is difficult to become trusted until your entire personal history has been laid out and dissected, until you have "shown yourself," and it is a handicap not to have relatives or friends or acquaintances already known, to whom your identity can be anchored. Names are treated almost sacredly and are not exchanged freely until that anchored relationship and trust have been established. Notes from early summer record: "Craig Bowman is the only person who calls me 'John.' No one else seems to call me anything unless they absolutely have to. In such forced circumstances, I am variously referred to as 'he' and 'him.' Who got that there ringer? He did. Whose turn is it? His'n. Everybody else is called by his first name."

Marion Pearsall gives the following examples of the importance of personal relations: "Whether a patient stays in a hospital or leaves against medical advice depends more on his personal relations with hospital personnel than on any understanding he may have of his medical condition and the hospital's technical competence in treating him. Similarly, parents decide they may 'let' their children go to school this year. Or a man enlists in the army as a favor to his country or goes to work on a given day in order to help the boss."[15]

In a research setting such as this, it is difficult to make the usual contact with informants because this is too shallow a relationship, too tenuous a bridge between two people to permit confident crossing. The role of researcher is therefore played down at first; in fact, it is necessary for the investigator first to play the informant while his biography is shyly, tentatively, and tediously drawn out by the people he wants to study. Then, as his interrogators move about more comfortably and begin to call him by name, the researcher can gradually turn the tables. This is a time-consuming but necessary phase of research into such subcultures. It is not wasted time, since the sensitive observer can learn much about his subjects from his own methodological problems. In this case, I learned that in some segments of the community, human relationships are not taken as lightly as I was used to; I learned this from my own experienced impatience.

This emphasis on the personal and the familiar in human relationships is hardly unique. Indeed it has been found so ubiquitously that together with its opposite—the cold, impersonal, utilitarian relationship—it forms a major axis of traditional social science theory.[16] Cooley would have referred to this kind of relationship as primary. Toennies designated it as *Gemeinschaft,* a kind of relationship based on natural will as opposed to rational will. It is the kind

[15] Pearsall, "Communicating with the Educationally Deprived," 11.

[16] See John C. McKinney and Charles P. Loomis, "The Application of Gemeinschaft and Gesellschaft as Related to Other Typologies," in the introduction to Ferdinand Toennies, *Community and Society,* ed. and trans. Charles P. Loomis (New York: Harper and Row, 1963), 12-29.

of relationship typical of Redfield's folk society, of Becker's sacred society, of Maine's status society, of Durkheim's mechanical society. It is what Sorokin would have classified as a familistic relation, and what Weber would have categorized as a mixture of affectual and traditional action orientations.

Perhaps the best-fitting concept to describe this value orientation is Gans' person-orientation, as opposed to object-orientation. The person-oriented individual values social relationships more than he does nonpersonal goals, such as income level, career, or a life style.[17] Similar in some ways are Parsons' pattern variables which guide basic choices in dilemmas of action. Specifically, relationships in this subculture tend to be affectively charged, particularistic, based on ascription, and defined diffusively.[18] Self-orientation appears to predominate in many contexts; this is related to what some observers have noted as the independence of the mountain man, which is sometimes romanticized into Thoreau-like self-sufficiency, and which Weller sees as individualism, which is more akin to selfishness.

"A man with independence may well work in his own way for a cooperative and common good," Weller writes. "Individualism, on the other hand, has a self-directed quality to it: a man works, perhaps in independent ways, with his own gain or well-being in mind. It is to this quality of individualism that the mountaineer's independence has come."[19] This quality helps explain the otherwise anomalous fact of widespread acceptance of and dependence on governmental programs of financial assistance by mountain families, an observation made by Pearsall, Weller, and Ford, and corroborated by my

[17] Gans, *The Urban Villagers,* 89-97.

[18] Talcott Parsons and Edward A. Shils, eds., *Toward a General Theory of Action* (Cambridge, Mass.: Harvard University Press, 1951).

[19] Weller, *Yesterday's People,* 30-31. Pearsall also refers to this value as individualism in *Little Smoky Ridge,* 4.

studies. So-called independence will be sold if the private gains are sufficient.

On the other hand, there is a difference between egotistic selfishness, a personality attribute, and individualism, a cultural doctrine. The individualist believes in generous, spontaneous charity to other individuals, as reflected in this informant's statement: "A man can't do for the whole community; he has to look out for himself and let the rest of the community look out for theirselves. Of course, if a man needs help, I'll help him—help him twice or help him three times—if he doesn't take advantage."

De Tocqueville has most nearly captured the essence of the mountain man's self-orientation in a passage linking individualism and democracy. There is a significant relationship to time-orientation, as has already been discussed, and an implicit explanation for the lack of success of sustained cooperative ventures.

> Egotism is a passionate and exaggerated love of self, which leads a man to connect everything with his own person, and to prefer himself to everything in the world. Individualism is a mature and calm feeling, which disposes each member of the community to sever himself from the mass of his fellow-creatures; and to draw apart with his family and his friends; so that, after he has thus formed a little circle of his own he willingly leaves society at large to itself. . . . Egotism blights the germ of all virtue; individualism, at first, only saps the virtues of public life. . . .
>
> As social conditions become more equal, the number of persons increases who, although they are neither rich enough nor powerful enough to exercise any great influence over their fellow-creatures, have nevertheless acquired or retained sufficient education and fortune to satisfy their own wants. They owe nothing to any man, they expect nothing from any man; they acquire the habit of always considering themselves as standing alone, and they are apt to

> imagine that their whole destiny is in their own hands. Thus not only does democracy make every man forget his ancestors, but it hides his descendants, and separates his contemporaries from him; it throws him back forever upon himself alone, and threatens in the end to confine him entirely within the solitude of his own heart.[20]

A relationship between this kind of independence and the value of personal relationships could also be argued for; indeed the traditional subculture seems to take on the shape of a functional unity. Independence, in this sense, means minding one's own business. This is a dictum more honored in the breach than in the observance—it is expected that a person will learn as much as he can about everyone else, but only so long as he does not misuse his knowledge. Minding one's own business is in turn a way of preserving relationships and achieving harmony. It is another way of saying, "Don't tell me what to do."

The willing dependence but assertive independence, which is typical of the traditional subculture, is characterized by a certain obstinancy, an unwillingness to acknowledge most authority, and a strong assertion that one is self-willed. Brenda Douglas echoes the sentiment in her blunt statement: "I don't tell anybody else what to do, and I don't want anybody telling me what to do." Kernodle refers to such people as the "last of the rugged individualists," and notes their decline in a community in western North Carolina.[21] There is a great reluctance among these mountain people to give directions, advice, or correction. There is an etiquette and a linquistic pattern encompassing this independence-harmony motif. For example, instead of saying, "You ought to see a doctor," it is more

[20] Alexis de Tocqueville, *Democracy in America* (New York: Colonial Press, 1899), Pt. II, Bk. 2, Chap. 2, pp. 104-106.

[21] R. Wayne Kernodle, "The Last of the Rugged Individualists," *Harper's Magazine* (Oct. 1960).

correct to say, "A person might drive over by Doc Hertz's." Instead of hearing, "You should change your ways," one hears, "A body ought to live right, don't you think?"

Just as no one wants to be dictated to, no one really wants to be under obligation to another person by receiving gifts or favors from him (this means being obliged, being beholden, or owing favors). This is because unwanted strings are often attached. There is a fear of having someone else "lord it over you."[22] For refusing—or at least accepting without loss of self-esteem—local acts of charity, mountain people have been called proud. The caseworker in the county seat says she admires something in the mountain man's spirit: "Some of them can accept welfare in a way that's gracious and even dignified. They aren't subservient." It may be significant, however, that few strings are attached to welfare recipiency.

Another trait commonly ascribed to the mountain culture of the past is familism. This trait appears to have been stronger in the mountains of eastern Kentucky than in this section of Appalachia, yet familism—a primary loyalty to family before any other group or principle—is to a degree characteristic of certain sectors of this community. There has not been the extent of family and clan feuding here as in Kentucky, but certain indications of familism, such as the tendency for siblings to stand together, the maintenance of family relationships over space and time, the existence of family work groups (particularly in the traditional occupations), and the prevalent social identification through kinship are nevertheless present.

Other writers and observers of the mountain people sometimes have appraised the traditional subculture in different terms than those I have used here, but none seem inconsistent with the dominant traits described, and, in fact, they reinforce my conclusions about broad sub-

[22] Pearsall, *Little Smoky Ridge,* 96.

cultural themes that stand at this pole in the total culture of Shiloh. Thus, for example, Weller, Ford, and others have referred to the mountain man as traditionalistic, which to Weller means, among other things, that "he does not look forward to tomorrow with pleasant anticipation." This term also means to Weller that the mountain man is existence-oriented.[23] These meanings of traditionalism indicate that it is closely related to the characteristic of shortened-time perspectives described earlier, and support the contention that people in this subculture live not much more in the past than they do in the future. The past is more a reinforcing myth, a palliative for the present, in the same way that Cash maintains the myth of the past works for the southern mind;[24] similarly, the fatalism that Ford notes as a dominant characteristic of lower socioeconomic status groups in the Southern Appalachians is described as contentment and/or resignation.[25]

The trait of action-seeking, which Weller borrows from Gans to apply to the mountain people, is part of the subcultural orientation to the present.[26] The "psychology of fear" did not appear to me to be so strong a culture trait as it did to Weller.[27]

Some writers have described the traditional mountain culture as having low standards of morality (primarily in the area of sexual behavior). Thus, Hannum describes a kind of Shakespearean moral laxity running throughout all strata of mountain society prior to the second quarter of this century.[28] Irregular unions are said not to have been uncommon in the past, she says, though attitudes

23 Weller, *Yesterday's People,* 34, 35.

24 W. J. Cash, *The Mind of the South* (New York: Knopf, 1960).

25 Thomas R. Ford, "The Passing of Provincialism," in *The Southern Appalachian Region: A Survey,* ed. Thomas R. Ford (Lexington: University of Kentucky Press, 1962), 15-21.

26 Weller, *Yesterday's People,* 40-43.

27 *Ibid.,* 44-49.

28 Alberta Pierson Hannum, "The Mountain People," in *The Great Smokies and the Blue Ridge,* ed. Roderick Peattie (New York: Vanguard Press, 1943), 83-85.

toward such unions and toward illegitimacy tightened as one went higher up on the social scale.

Likewise Hartman says that in the community of Newland, unmarried mothers were not looked down on but were rather pitied, unless a girl maintained a consistent pattern of illegitimacy. Like Hannum writing in 1943, Hartman observes of the period 1947–1948 that attitudes of higher-status individuals in the community have become increasingly critical.[29] According to an informant in Shiloh, attitudes toward such things as illegitimacy have not altered from these descriptions: "There are a lot of bastards around here—more than you would think. But it's a funny thing: people here don't care as much about it, they don't look down on a person as much as they would other places. They more or less accept him like they would anybody else." Campbell cites the work of Fiske, who maintains that the North Carolina frontier was made up of inept entrepreneurs and outright outlaws emigrating from Virginia.[30] According to Fiske, these mean whites found life easier in the ruder society of the frontier. He cites the governor of Virginia as saying in 1717: "The inhabitants of our frontiers are composed generally of such as have been transported hither as servants, and being out of their time, . . . settle themselves where Land is to be taken up . . . that will produce the necessarys of Life with little Labour. It is pretty well known what Morals such people bring with them hither, which are not like to be much mended by their Scituation [*sic*], remote from all places of worship."[31] Thomas has noted of the older mountain society that everybody's morals were divorced from religion.[32]

[29] Hartman, "A Cultural Study," 241-44.

[30] John C. Campbell, *The Southern Highlander and His Homeland* (New York: Russell Sage Foundation, 1921), 349-51. Neither Campbell nor Kephart wholly accepts this theory.

[31] Cited by Fiske in *ibid.*, 350.

[32] W. R. Thomas, *Life Among the Hills and Mountains of Kentucky* (Louisville: Standard Printing Co., 1926).

Whether these standards of morality are applicable to the traditional subculture in contemporary Shiloh is difficult to demonstrate, but from the available evidence it appears there is among some traditionalists a certain theme of openness or relative freedom of restraint in sexual matters. In conversation among a male and a female informant and me on the lady's front porch one afternoon she casually observed that she could "have more fun with a married man than she could with these young boys." She said the advantage of going out with married men was that they wouldn't tell on you. The man declared, "I'm fifty-five right now, and I like it better now'n I did when I was sixteen. Yeah, I really like it now." But he said his wife wouldn't let him get close to her. One man from nearby told me: "I tell you this woman business is really something. It isn't worth all the trouble and worry it brings. There isn't a woman stacked, nor built, nor beautified enough to make it worth it. I quit it, and I'm glad; it'd have to be some kind of a nice setup before I would do it again. There's an awful lot of it goes on around here, though." He went on to tell of a number of illicit relationships of which he knew.

At another time I was told of several runaways (in which a man and a woman abscond together) which had occurred in Shiloh in recent years. And once during the summer, in a place near Spartown, a married service-station owner, one of a group of three men, was shot and critically wounded by the father of a young girl the men had come to visit. The men had been drinking. The father is said to have warned them to leave the premises several times, then fired at them. The visit, according to a well-informed person, was planned for illicit purposes.

Activities such as these may be related to the value theme of individualism, in that it seems to involve a partial rejection of obligation and responsibility and a positive valuation of freedom from restraint. It might be argued that these traits are responses to the contemporary situation rather than simple cultural hand-me-downs. It could be argued that premarital pregnancies result from aggressive behavior on the part of young people frustrated by environmental deprivation, or that alternative modes of dating, courtship, and relating to the opposite sex are blocked for certain segments of the community. Perhaps adulterous relationships are established as a means of escaping unrewarding marital situations set up in thoughtless, youthful haste and maintained in a degrading atmosphere of dulling poverty. These arguments are correct, but only in part. The situational demands are there, to be sure, but so are the cultural remnants of a past way of life which people inherit and reshape as tools to solve the adaptive problems of their era. Thus, the final outcome—the existing traditional value themes and other cultural traits—is a blend of responses to present demands and past culture.

In describing the dominant themes of the traditional subculture, it is necessary to touch again on one very noticeable feature: the sharp differences, in certain respects, between the worlds of men and women. Apparent first of all is the physical separateness between the sexes. During the day, men and women are engaged in activities that remove them from each other's company. Even when families go galacking together, the men pick together in one place and the women pick together in another place. In the evenings, the men are frequently away from the house in search of coon, possum, or strong drink, while the women stay home.[33] Again, though whole families may attend church together (many don't), they tend to segregate themselves by sex once they arrive at the door: the women and young children go inside and the men hang

[33] As Leighton says, "While the men fish, the women fume." See Dorothea Leighton and others, *The Character of Danger* (New York: Basic Books, 1963), 367.

back and form conversational groups in the churchyard until the last minute. Once inside, the men frequently take seats across the aisle from the women or in the all-male amen corner. In one service I attended, there were forty-four people seated on the left, of which one was a man and six were boys. Thirty were seated on the right, of which only four were women.

In addition to this spatio-temporal distinctness, there are differences in outlook and attitude. In spite of the fact that the outward form of the traditional family in the mountains is strongly patriarchal, and in spite of the fact that in these families a man—because he is a man, nothing else—is lord in his house, it cannot be said that a woman is simply a passive, subordinate reflection of her husband's attitudes and wants. She may be subordinate in some ways, and her public countenance may dutifully mirror her man's outlook on a wide range of matters. But in more intimate surroundings, she gives indications that the goals she has in mind for her family are different from those of her man, that she really wishes life were organized with different values in mind. In a word, it seems that women more frequently than men aspire to achieve what they consider a higher rung, a better life. They appear less satisfied with the status quo. In a survey conducted in the county by a state antipoverty group among low-income (under $3,000), rural, "whole-family" respondents, 42 percent of the male respondents indicated satisfaction with housing while only 29 percent of the female respondents had no complaints.[34]

The women tend to nag their men in private, not necessarily with a clear view to pushing them up the social ladder, but with this net effect if the men were to heed the unasked advice. One night I noticed that Hope was pouting at John Henry and asked him if she were mad at him. He said:

[34] Data from North Carolina Fund Socioeconomic Survey, conducted in 1965. *N* on which the statement above is based is 141.

> Naw, she ain't mad. A little upset, maybe. See, she thinks I ought to work all the time, Thinks I ought to work eight hours a day and then come home and work and do things and just set around the house or do what she thinks I ought to do. Now if you was to be around our house 365 days out of the year, you'd see that as long as I did that everything would be just fine. But when I try to have a little sociable life of my own, when I come home and do what *I* want to do, she don't like that.

There seems to be almost a constant battle of the sexes, a battle in which the participants use so much camouflage it seems more like guerrilla warfare than open warfare. Sometimes women enlist the aid of their children in guiding their husbands into living better. They also frequently use religion and the church as instruments of reform; to persuade a man to lead a saintly life is to move toward domesticating him, and the domestication of the male is a good first step upward for the whole family.

John C. Campbell noted that men and women are socialized differently, have different spheres of activity, and are judged by different standards.[35] Some of his observations suggest that male authority did not always go undisputed by mountain women. Hannum likewise comments that "despite their submission, mountain women, like women the world over, have their little ways."[36] One is reminded of the observations made by Hu Shih regarding the Chinese family, cited in an essay by Ping-ti Ho: "At the outset, it is necessary to point out that the position of women in the old family was never so low as many superficial observers have led us to believe. On the contrary, woman has always been the despot of the family. The authority of the mother and the mother-in-law is very well known. Even the wife is always the terror of the

[35] Campbell, *The Southern Highlander,* 126-27, 136-37. See also Pearsall, *Little Smoky Ridge,* 88 ff.

[36] Hannum, "The Mountain People," 127.

husband; no other country in the world can compete with China for the distinction of being the nation of henpecked husbands."[37] These statements are extreme even for the Chinese family, and they are certainly out of proportion for the Southern Appalachian family, but they are antidotes to the dominant view of the traditional mountain family as a strict, albeit benign, tyranny by the male. On the whole, however, the men can be said to seek more after contentment and immediate satisfaction while the women are rather more concerned with betterment. The men tend to look backward and into the present, the women into the future.

What comes across to the observer as *the* value orientations of the traditional subculture are probably more those of the men than the women in this segment of the community. Doubtless this impression of singularity of values is fostered because it is the man who is the official spokesman of family policy in most of these families. He does most of the talking, and the family attitudes one assays in a given situation are mostly his and not necessarily those of the whole family. Usually it is only in the more relaxed and familiar settings that the woman (and sometimes the children) expresses her views of the world and allows the publicly disavowed differences between herself and her husband to be known.

The second and more recently arrived subculture of Shiloh might be called the contemporary, the outside, or the modern. The value themes and orientations referred to under this rubric are not simply contemporary and do not have all their origins outside the mountain area. There have long been strains in mountain society, espe-

[37] Ping-ti Ho, "An Historian's View of the Chinese Family System," in *Man and Civilization: The Family's Search for Survival,* ed. Seymour Farber, Piero Mustacchi, and Roger H. L. Wilson (New York: McGraw-Hill, 1965), 23-24.

cially in more heavily populated areas such as the county seats, which were highly sympathetic with, if not actually expressive of, societal patterns in the outside world.[38] In more rural areas, this element of mountain society has been represented primarily by the local storekeepers and native teachers. The historical trend might be compared to a narrow stream that trickles along for miles and suddenly widens out and courses rapidly as it is joined by huge tributaries from outside. After a certain point it is difficult to say what part is the original stream and what part has been brought in. At least it is clear that the outside world is not as alien to mountain communities as many historians and journalists have unintentionally led us to conclude. "Basic change occurs only, or usually, when the seeds of it, almost always located *outside* the system, fall upon the fertile soil which the variations *within* the system provide."[39]

The statement that this subculture is contemporary must be elaborated by saying that it is contemporary, urban, and middle-class.[40] There are other cultures contemporary with this one but different from it—such as those characteristic of rural America and the urban lower class.[41]

Another matter regarding use of a term like this one (and others such as *Gesellschaft,* organic, and urban) con-

[38] Campbell, *The Southern Highlander,* 80-81: "We shall in the course of this study have little occasion to refer to this part of the mountain population, whose characteristics and problems are on the whole not different from those of groups living in similar places in other parts of the United States and who need little assistance save as all groups need touch with the forces working for social advancement." Kephart likewise distinguishes among townfolk, valley farmers, and "real mountaineers," concentrating on the last to the exclusion of the others. See Kephart, *Our Southern Highlanders,* preface and p. 287. Analyses that concentrate only on the traditional or that place the traditional only in rural settings and the modern only in "town" settings, fail to appreciate the great range of cultural variations existing side by side in places like Shiloh.

[39] Kluckhohn and Strodtbeck, *Variations in Value Orientations,* 45.

[40] Descriptions of urban "middle-class" value orientations which I have in mind are ones found in such social science "classics" as Warner, Hollingshead, the Lynds, and so forth.

[41] See Gans, *The Urban Villagers,* 230-42.

cerns its relationships to its antithetical terms (such as archaic or traditional, *Gemeinschaft,* mechanical, or folk). One fact that Howard Odum underscored in his regional sociology was that the folk, the soul of a people, does not necessarily become lost simply because it becomes urbanized. The folk remains as a substratum over which urban thoughtways, stateways, and technicways are laid.[42] Carstens makes the same point when he warns against employing a false dichotomy between folk and urban types in community studies.[43] The Toennies approach to the study of society too often assumes that primary relations decrease in number and importance in complex societies; this assumption is probably not justified, according to Carstens —it is merely that the extent of secondary contacts may increase.

From a different vantage point, but still pertinent to the issue, Blumer points out that social scientists studying industrialization have assumed only one possible response of the traditional order in the face of change: resistance. He proceeds to offer five possible alternative consequences of the introduction of industrialization into a traditional order, and concludes that all of them may occur simultaneously in different segments of the same society. Blumer rejects a dichotomous approach and allows for different types of confluence of traditional and modern ways of life.[44]

Weintraub and Bernstein bring data to bear from two villages in Israel which demonstrate Blumer's point.[45]

42 Katherine Jocher and others, *Folk, Region, and Society: Selected Papers of Howard Odum* (Chapel Hill: University of North Carolina Press, 1964), 223-24.

43 Peter Carstens, "Anthropological Aspects of the Community," John W. Umstead Lectures in Community Mental Health (unpublished paper, University of North Carolina, Raleigh, Feb. 1965).

44 Herbert Blumer, "Industrialization and the Traditional Order," *Sociology and Social Research,* XLVIII (Jan. 1964), 129-38.

45 D. Weintraub and F. Bernstein, "Social Structure and Modernization: A Comparative Study of Two Villages," *American Journal of Sociology,* LXXI (March 1966), 509-21.

These authors feel that the two villages are matched on all important characteristics except response to modernization and kinship structure, and they interpret the differential response as heavily influenced by the type of kinship: in one village, the traditional kinship structure helped to produce some modernizing trends. These data "lend support to the view that the 'opposing' principles of traditionalism and modernity are not as mutually exclusive as has often been assumed, and that not only can they co-exist under certain conditions, but that they may even reinforce one another."[46]

Other empirical evidence that indirectly supports critics of mutual exclusion of tradition and modernism is supplied by Litwak's studies of the modified extended family, which offer data contrary to the hypothesis of Parsons and others that industrialization brings a concomitant, functionally suitable nuclearization of the family.[47] Litwak finds that certain features of the extended family typical of nonmobile, nonurbanized folk sectors of society are maintained even through extensive mobility and urbanization. He suggests—and his suggestion has been very widely accepted—that we have oversimplified the picture by assuming only two basic family types and a corresponding functional incompatibility between the two.

An observer in Shiloh would be unable to find a clearly defined separation between traditional and modern ways of life. The new is overlaid on the old; the old incorporates the new. Thus, although the following description emphasizes the new and draws attention to departures from the

[46] *Ibid.*, 521.

[47] Eugene Litwak, "Occupational Mobility and Extended Family Cohesion," *American Sociological Review*, XXV (Feb. 1960), 9-21; Eugene Litwak, "Geographical Mobility and Extended Family Cohesion," *American Sociological Review*, XXV (June 1960), 385-94. See also the critical discussions of the "fit" between industrialization and the nuclear family in William Goode, *World Revolution and Family Pattern* (Glencoe, Ill.: Free Press, 1963), and in Wilbert Moore, *Social Change* (New York: Prentice-Hall, 1963).

so-called traditional way of life, it should be borne in mind that there are points of commonality between the two, and that the new is sometimes like a thin coat of paint on an old house: the original texture still shows through in places. Ab Cooper, for example, is a storekeeper who earnestly desires to make it big in the tourist business, but who wants things left in their natural state: "Tell you the truth, though, I'd just as soon there's not be any boom around here. I don't want a bunch of people coming up here and spoiling these mountains. I like it the way it is." This kind of ambivalence between the traditional and the modern subcultures is common.

If the atmosphere of the traditional subculture is one of contentment, satisfaction, and doing without, then the prevailing winds of the modern subculture are more heavily laden with dissatisfaction and striving. The following notes made on a sermon delivered in a modernist Baptist church express the typical attitude toward work and the contrast with traditional attitudes:

> At one place in the sermon, the preacher exhorted the congregation to make the best they could of themselves. "Everybody ought to strive to be the best he can," etc. (A dash of Protestant ethic.) This aspect of "works" was not found in Freedom Chapel [fundamentalist], where "works" means "living right," i.e., not lying, not drinking, not stealing, not committing adultery, and the like. It's not what you do so much as what you don't do that counts. The only positive action required for salvation is getting the spirit once in a while. In the "downtown" Baptist church, there is a glimmer of something else.

Two goals appear to be paramount: monetary success and a high prestige standing in the local community. Ab Cooper would like to make it big and has ideas for capitalizing on the tourist business and building a rest home for the elderly, in addition to owning part of a store and being a heavy equipment operator. Ernest Phelps and Craig Bowman care enough about the present and future of their store businesses to keep monthly accounts and compare them with previous years. Craig even charts his accounts. Moreover, he keeps up with the stock market and has definite opinions on the future of the national economy. Craig operates a logging concern and raises tobacco in addition to running a store with his father, and he has recently ventured into real estate speculation. He described his attitude toward money: "I'm money-crazy, like Jack Snyder says. . . . It's not that I would enjoy having a lot of money—I just enjoy getting it. It's the fun of making it. Last night I spent three-quarters of an hour on the phone and got the mineral rights to my new property, which makes it worth five or ten times more. People told me I couldn't get them, and Dad said I'd have to pay more than I did pay. I was so elated I couldn't sleep all night." Craig's hobby is coin-collecting.

Ford says of the entire Southern Appalachian Region: "Most of the people of the Region, according to the evidence of the survey data, have adopted the major goals and standards typical of American society. They, like other people throughout the nation, wish to have larger incomes, greater material comforts, and more prestigeful status."[48]

Barely subordinated to these goals, perhaps, is the desire for standing not only among local friends and acquaintances, but for the respect and the attention—or at least not the ridicule—of persons outside the community and outside the region. Charles Shores is an exaggerated example of a man who really wants to appear successful:

> At one point, Charles said mountain people like himself were poor and ignorant. He was explaining that

[48] Ford, "The Passing of Provincialism," 32.

> he resented (as everybody else did) Florida people coming up here and showing their money and education and pushing people around. (One may need go no further in looking for Charles' motives for climbing.) Later, however, he gave the impression, without saying anything definite, that he had more education than most around here, and that he was worth more than most.
>
> He showed the view . . . and pointed out his place. By the sweep of his hand, it appeared that he owned a major portion of the great stretch in front of us. Actually, one could see only a small portion of the four or five acres his brother sold him years ago.

Some of the residences might well be regarded as advertisements for the self, as, for example, in the case of this family: "The house is old, but substantially remodeled. It is relatively small, but richly landscaped and decorated on the inside: garden statues, oriental wind-chimes, shrubs, trees, flowers, garden furniture on the outside; richly upholstered chairs, antique pieces, hundreds of green plants, lace tablecloth, modern kitchen inside. The house is one of few in the area with a central furnace." It is significant that after a discussion of social levels in the community, the lady of this house inquired obliquely how I thought they rated; a similar incident occurred with a different couple.

To pursue this latter goal requires a partial repudiation of traditional mountain life, since to gain the respect and to avoid the ridicule of outsiders necessitates breaking out of habits, tastes, mannerisms, and attitudes that the striving mountain person believes is part of the stereotype of the mountaineer held by the outsider. A person in this category resents references to mountain dwellers as hillbillies or mountaineers and tends to play down the differences between mountain people and people anywhere else. Many residents of the community enjoy the cartoon strip "Snuffy Smith," but they deplore the fact that for outlanders this is one of the few sources of information about life in the mountains. An observation in the field notes from early July says: "There is a natural resentment here against stereotypes held by the outlander. The source of these stereotypes is held to be hillbilly books and movies and Snuffy Smith cartoons. Most of the expression of this resentment takes a joking form, and comes from the upper group in the community. But everybody, bottom to top, enjoys a joke about what city people, flatlanders, slickers, etc., think of mountain people. The increasing number of tourists in this vicinity has doubtless heightened self-awareness; more people are looking in the looking glass."

One story I recall hearing took place at a roadside cider-and-honey stand that was manned by an ordinary-looking mountain resident dressed in ordinary-looking clothes. A tourist from Pennsylvania pulled up, got out, looked over the merchandise and the native entrepreneur, and asked, "Where are all these mountaineers I've been hearing about? I thought they were all barefooted, bearded, and carried a jug and a dog and a gun with them." The mountain man stepped out from behind his stand and glanced at the tourist's license. "Don't know for certain," he is said to have replied, "but they tell me they all went to Pennsylvania to teach school."

Mrs. Greene volunteered a similar story which makes light of the nonmountaineer's ignorance of modern Appalachia.

> Have you heard about the time a carload from California pulled up at the information booth on the square in Asheville? The driver asked where they could see some real hillbillies, and the man in the booth said, "Yes, I can tell you where to see one. Just turn left at the next corner and then turn left again

> and then make two left turns. Can't miss him." The car came back in about five minutes and the driver said, "Hey, we're back where we started from." The man said, "You said you wanted to see a hillbilly—well, I'm as much of a hillbilly as any you'll find around here."

Another example of this sensitivity to outsiders' stereotypes is Frank Harmon's reaction to a bottling company's new advertising campaign in which the product was billed as a hillbilly drink. The essence of his feeling was that he didn't care if he was a hillbilly, he just didn't want anybody calling him that.

Craig Bowman asked me one day if I planned to disguise the locale of the study. I explained to him that this was assumed as part of the ethics of research and as fair turnabout for people who had been so much help during the study. "Nobody," I said "wants a bunch of people coming up here asking where's the old man that said such-and-such, and all that." He said, "Like that *National Geographic* article and *Home on the Ridge*?"[49] I said, "Yes, exactly like that." He said Zeb McCall didn't appreciate being photographed in his overalls, even though he wears them all the time. I agreed that no one wanted to be told he was colorful and picturesque.

The modernist holds in low regard the journalists who travel to the remotest coves in search of local color and poverty, and who play up the backwardness of places like Shiloh. He knows there is backwardness, ignorance, dirt, bad housing, and characters by the dozen, but he knows there is also himself, who is never interviewed.

The repudiation of tradition extends to speech patterns, dress, leisure activities, friendships, kin relations, religion, housing, and numerous folkways of consumption. Craig

[49] Pseudonym for a book written several years ago which included parts of the study area, and about which many local people are sensitive because they feel it portrays them as "backward."

Bowman noted, regarding dress, that "overalls and work-shoes are a sign of outdoor work; the men in industrial jobs will tend to wear slacks and slippers." Women are careful not to wear clothes that appear tacky. Concerning use of leisure, although some men who are modernists still enjoy hunting and fishing, many, like Charles Shores, feel that they don't have the time to engage in such fruitless pastimes. Charles is also a man who seems to have repudiated friendships and kin ties in his desire to become modern: "Don't even none of his brothers come by to see him, except to aggravate him."[50]

In the area of consumption, the mass arts provide a good example of repudiation. This region has one of the richest heritages of folklore—folksongs, crafts, folktales, folk dances, games—but a real poverty of indigenous exploiters of this highly valued national commodity. In the local talent shows one would expect to hear many of the famous ballads collected by Cecil Sharp, or at least some hand-me-down gospel songs, but, instead, he hears mostly poor renditions of the top ten jukebox favorites. Meanwhile, professional songsters from New York, California, and elsewhere are raking the hills collecting songs, taking them back home and presenting them to audiences hungry for roots and nostalgic for something they never knew. It is an interesting and significant form of cultural exchange in which the youth of the region reach out for what they see as modernity and the youth outside reach back for the exotica of an archaic world.

One further incident recorded in the field notes symbolizes this reaching out for a more modern, urban life: "I put a coin in the nickel jukebox at the grill today and told the thirteen- or fourteen-year-old boy next to me to play whatever he wanted to hear. He played a tune . . .

[50] See James S. Brown, "The Conjugal Family and the Extended Family Group," *American Sociological Review,* XVII (June 1952), 297-306, where he describes familial strains frequently ranging around "class differences."

called 'Downtown,' which claims that one's troubles all vanish when one goes downtown."

There is a certain self-consciousness that goes along with costuming oneself in new cultural robes: the self-consciousness and thinly veiled defensiveness of the nouveau. This too-careful guarding of the image is a distinctive mark of the mountain person who has begun to turn his back on tradition (which is now suspect as a generator and maintainer of a degrading stereotype) and who is beginning to plunge into the mainstream of American culture.

As with the traditional subculture, however, the modern subculture is not simply negative, i.e., not simply a repudiation of some other way of life. It has its own positive goals and values and means for achieving them, its own standards of good and personal worth, and its own ultimate concerns. Monetary success, community respect, and acceptance as "our kind" by representatives of the outside world are examples of commanding positive goals. The means to these goals affect the resultant life style of modernists just as the means to achieving a sense of contentment and at-homeness set the life styles of traditionalists.

Thus, consumption patterns sometimes have a Veblenesque tone of conspicuousness. Things are bought for the sake of their appearance, and not simply because they are needed. Craig admitted that his old car was really in good shape and that he traded simply because he wanted a bigger, newer car. Charles Shores pointed proudly to his riding mower and said, "There's not many around here like that." The only Thunderbird in town is Mrs. Greene's; the recent-vintage Buicks all belong to modernists, and so on.

Thus also, one can sense a strain toward constant change which is a symptom of a culture partially based on planned (and unplanned) obsolescence. Not only in the case of material goods but also with the consumption of less tangible cultural fashions such as music, humor, fashions of speech, and products of mass culture, there is found in some segments of Shiloh an ardent desire to keep up. Although keeping up, staying with the times, and being "in" are valued positively, these goals are tinged with a latent fear of being backward and of revealing some remote kinship with the Snuffy Smith element.

Likewise, attitudes toward work and education indicate that in the modern subculture they are viewed primarily as means to ends and as respect-bestowing achievements in themselves. The work ethic is strong in this subculture. Where there is a tendency in the traditional subculture to carry over life into work, there is an opposite tendency to separate life and work in the modern subculture; whereas in the former, life is the hands-down winner over work, in the latter, work tends to predominate over life as a central concern. The job has thus become very important to some people in Shiloh. To live without working is to be accounted worthless, "no-count." This characteristic attitude is to be contrasted with the view in the traditional subculture that work is more or less necessary for getting by and should be made an enjoyable pastime insofar as it is possible. Not to have to work is often to be counted lucky. Charles Shores is typical of the modernist in having nothing but contempt for "nail-keg guys" (loafers). Clarence Haskell represents the traditionalists with his view that a man must work only because he has to.

There also appear to be certain subsidiary social components of this movement toward the Protestant ethic, often clustered into the single term *adaptability*. Typical of this frame of mind are these lines from a letter written by Frank Proffitt, late of Watauga County, North Carolina: "My life is now and always has been one of constant changes and adaptations. No one with a 'planned life' from birth could understand anything other than a 'set pattern.' No such life existed for me, nor does it now."[51] One component of adaptability is an ability or a willingness to tolerate ambiguity and uncertainty regarding the future. The willingness to risk is an essential trait of entrepreneurship and status advancement generally, and the enjoyment of risk-taking found sometimes in the modern sector of Shiloh contrasts with the value of stability found in the traditional subculture. One man who never really "went modern" in terms of life style nevertheless demonstrates this aspect of adaptability; here is how Marcus Eller (now deceased) described his life:

> Well, I started off in the mining business. Sometimes I didn't do so well; I didn't always make good. Mica started going bad after awhile, and I decided that I would start raising cattle. I bought me a young bull out in Kansas, the son of a grand champion bull. I bought another'n from out in Missouri. Pretty soon I had about the best-looking cattle anywhere. Some people will tell you, there ain't nothing, no work, to raising cattle. That's a mistake. I begin to sell them off and pretty soon I sold the last one I had. A few people followed suit in cattle, but not many.
>
> About that time, the government had bought up some property near here and done some mining on it, and I heard they was getting ready to sell some of it. Wasn't many people had much confidence in that land as I had, but I decided I wanted it, so I wrote somebody in the federal government about it. I guess it was a year later, some man in the federal land bank wrote and said they was a man coming who would sell that land to the highest bidder. He come by and I made him a price. He left and come back in a couple of days and said somebody had raised my bid. That went on for a long time, and looked like it wouldn't

[51] Cited by Cratis D. Williams in "Frank Proffitt, 1913–1965," *Mountain Life and Work* (Spring 1966), 7.

> stop. But that other feller had only been raising $25 ever time and I had been raising a hundred, so the man said I could have it. I didn't have enough money to pay for it all, so I went to my cashier. I told him I didn't have enough money. He said if you want it then bid any damn thing you want on it. He's a nice feller, that cashier. So I got the property. I leased some of it for mining. I own a right big lot around here. It wouldn't fetch too much right now, but it will in a few years.

Another component closely related is the willingness to defer gratification, a trait found lacking by some students of lower-class life, and one that is not often found among partakers of tradition in Shiloh. This is not to say that persons who have committed themselves to the modern way of life are perfectly disciplined and always able to subordinate immediate wishes to long-range goals with higher ultimate payoff. But deferred gratification is much more highly developed in the modern subculture than in the traditional.

The third related component of this adaptability trait concerns time perspective or orientation. The traditional subculture is oriented primarily to the present, and to a certain extent to the past, a factor related to the unwillingness to defer gratification. The modern subculture is much more oriented to the future, and this ability or willingness to enjoy the future before it arrives helps account for the concomitant willingness to put off immediate rewards in favor of expected long-term gains. People most committed to the modern way of life, for example, are willing to invest money in long-term business ventures, encourage children to spend long years in school, and forego the many opportunities for "loafering around," hunting and fishing, playing hookey, spending money on passing fancies, and so forth. They will put in regular working hours and sometimes take on extra jobs, feeling that "a man that lives in these parts has to work like I do to get ahead: find work every hour instead of wasting time." Charles Shores said that he would not have time to talk to me because he was busy working (this was Sunday morning), but that if he could, he would be of more help than "some of these people that sits around on nail kegs all day." (That this man was not entirely successful in postponing immediate desires in favor of pecuniary success is attested to by the fact that he was somewhat intoxicated at the time of this exchange.) Lawrence Harmon mused one day about the difference between himself and a lot of people who don't seem to be able to make a good life, "I just worked along and always tried to save. I guess you'd say the difference was in looking ahead. A lot of people just don't look ahead, they live from one day to the next." Marcus Eller agreed. "I guess," he said, "you could call it good management and foresight."

Another contrast between modern and traditional subcultures is found on the dimension of human relationships and their meanings. Traditionalists consider trust as essential in relating to others; familiarity (through longstanding acquaintance, kinship, or an informal system of references) lay the necessary groundwork for building rapport. The network of relationships among traditionalists is relatively low-scale and limited more or less to primary bonds among family, neighbors, and friends. Most of the people with whom a participant in this subculture comes into contact will be part of a relationship that is an end in itself. The important exceptions to this general statement are people such as nonlocal merchants, social workers and other agency representatives, tourists and summer people.

Many relationships in the modern subculture, on the other hand, are of relatively higher scale and of a more secondary nature. There are still important primary ties involving relatively intense, frequent, intrinsically rewarding interactions with family and friends, but there are other relationships that extend beyond these, both in the sense of locale and intimacy or primariness. In this subculture there is greater likelihood that a relationship will be treated not simply as an end in itself but as a means to something else; for example, as a means to information, as a means to greater prestige through association, as an instrument in the acquisition of goods, property, or money, and as a source of advice. In sum, any single relationship in this subculture is more likely than one in the traditional subculture to exist on both primary and secondary levels, and, furthermore, of the total number of relationships people establish with one another, a higher proportion are likely to be of a secondary nature in the modern subculture. Here human beings are more likely to be related to and evaluated on the basis of instrumentality than familiarity.

Identification of a stranger is more likely to be accomplished through the question *What* are you? than through the question *Who* are you? It would, of course, be a mistake to think that relationships involved in the modern subculture were remarkably pure specimens of utilitarianism. They are not remarkable at all in this respect, but are simply closer to urban, *Gesellschaft,* secular, organic, contract, rational, object-oriented, affectively neutral, universalistic, achievement-based, specific relationships than are relationships in the traditional subculture.

Somewhat less extreme is the contrast between the two subcultures on the dimension of self-orientation versus collectivity-orientation. With certain exceptions, the traditional subculture is by and large classifiable as self-oriented. The exceptions are family and to some extent church. The orientation in the modern subculture seems to be somewhat more toward the collective, but not yet a great deal. Kernodle, writing of changes taking place in another area of the mountains, finds that one of the most notable changes from prewar days is the one away from individualism toward living within the framework of various collectives: businesses, PTA's, garden clubs, and the like.[52] In Shiloh there are not many voluntary associations to which to belong, and there are no joiners, supposed by some to be typical of middle-class America. But it is true that if anyone in Shiloh belongs to the PTA (organized, incidentally, by relative newcomers from the urban north in an adjacent community), he is probably a modernist. Members of the county chamber of commerce, holders of season tickets (seldom used) to a nearby imported summer stock theater, members of the Coon Club recently brought into being in the next county (incredibly but significantly, this is a rational, "modern," formal organization dedicated to the preservation and encouragement of an ancient traditional sport enjoyed because of its spontaneous, nonrational nature by men who didn't have to be awake at work the next morning), and members of the few other such groups are also likely to be at or heading toward modernism.

Yet, on the other hand, there are very few business partnerships; every man who wants to be in business would rather be in business for himself. There is little inclination toward cooperative group action and very little background training for such cooperation, as Weller noted about West Virginia mountain dwellers. Cooperation works as long as it is spontaneous, as long as everyone involved is motivated toward the same end, and as long as everyone feels he is getting his due. But even modernists seem unable to hold together in a formal organization for very long; when it has served whatever immediate purpose it was organized for, it tends to atomize again. Thus, active PTA membership dropped considerably after the initial membership drive was over. A community development club, organized in 1953, failed to survive longer than a year. Town signs were erected but were not replaced when the wind blew them down. Active political party membership follows the same pattern; except for a few

[52] Kernodle, "The Last of the Rugged Individualists."

activists, and despite the ardent partisan feelings of almost every voting man in Shiloh, there is no political organization but the phoenixlike election machinery that rises from its ashes every two or four years.

The necessary condition of unanimity of motive or purpose for the survival of such organizations in Shiloh may be explained by the fact that few people in the community seem to have learned the art of compromise, or the ability temporarily to put aside or submerge irrelevant differences in order collectively to pursue other goals. The possibility of coalition is enhanced when people are easily able to segment each other and relate to each other in a contractual way; although this talent is more fully developed in the modern subculture than in the traditional subculture of Shiloh, it is still in its latency period. Thus, a voluntary association formed in this community is likely to be made up of people who are fairly like-minded in *many* respects and not just the respect that is the *raison d'être* of the group. In this community, even friendships have been known to dissolve over disagreements as to the relative merits of Fords and Chevrolets.

The case of the county merchants association, which was established to put sanctions on poor credit risks, will perhaps suffice to show what happens when participants in an organization do not feel they are getting their due. Actually, they may be getting what they bargained for, but the rewards of cooperative endeavor in many groups are relatively long-range ones, and they require giving up accustomed shortrun gains. All merchants were to pool names of customers who met a certain criterion of bad credit, share the list among themselves, and refuse to extend credit to anyone whose name was on the list. This arrangement was to stop the practice of customers' running up credit with one merchant until he would sell no more, then going to another merchant down the road and running up a sizable bill with him until he cut off credit, and so on. A man could make the rounds for quite a few years in this way before he had to start ranging out farther for credit. The fact is that he still can, because the merchants association plan failed. The reason for the failure, one merchant explained, was because when a new customer came in asking for credit, the storekeepers wanted to keep him as a customer and were afraid some other store would break the code and get him themselves. Even though he might be known as a bad credit risk, he *might* start paying this time, and the storekeeper would have lost. An additional reason is that storekeepers have always been relatively free with credit because they were dealing with friends and neighbors, not just economic objects, and the traditional desire to stand in favor with one's fellows exerted a strong pull.

In the past, it might be argued, there may be found numerous examples of collective endeavor which indicate an inconsistent cultural theme when placed alongside the many instances of independence and individualism to be found. There are many examples of "neighboring," a tradition that still survives in certain forms, mainly as borrowing (or stealing), in the traditional subculture. Barn raisings, house raisings, housewarmings, cornhuskings, tobacco-hangings, woodchoppings, and quilting bees are things for which the region has become famous, but they are things of the past. Even in the past, though, they were spontaneous short-lived gatherings which did not require any great sacrifice, cooperation, or the sustaining of long-term organization. Even in 1922, Kephart noted, "Neighborliness has not grown in the mountains—it is on the wane. There are today fewer log-rollings and house-raisings, fewer husking bees and quilting parties than in former times; *and no new social gatherings have taken their place.*"[53] A summer's fieldwork revealed a few instances of new forms of collectives, mostly found in the

[53] Kephart, *Our Southern Highlanders,* 382-83.

traditional subculture. Borrowing of tools, food, money, whiskey, and beer took place, but usually among kin. Neighbors or friends sometimes helped to harvest tobacco crops, but they were always paid something for their work; it was sometimes difficult to get even family members to help out in the fields and barns. Bridal and baby showers are not unknown to the community, but none took place during June–September 1965. Men's and women's softball teams were organized during the summer for the first time in the community. Teenagers and adult men and women from several levels of the community formed, impromptu and without benefit of leadership, teams which played neighboring village teams weekly and which practiced almost nightly as long as the enthusiasm lasted (about one month).

But generally, the words of Kephart hold true for both subcultures of Shiloh; the situation has changed only just noticeably.

> The mountaineers are non-social. As they stand today, each man "fighting for his own hand, with his back against the wall," they recognize no social compact. Each one is suspicious of the other. Except as kinsmen or partisans they cannot pull together. Speak to them of community of interests, try to show them the advantages of cooperation, and you might as well be proffering advice to the North Star. They will not work together zealously even to improve their neighborhood roads, each mistrusting that the other may gain some trifling advantage over himself or turn fewer shovelfuls of earth.[54]

Some of the local citizens attribute difficulties in sustained cooperative endeavor to lack of leadership, which is a true but incomplete explanation. The leadership problem results from a holdover, even among modernists, of

[54] *Ibid.*, 383.

the value of harmonious personal relations in the traditional mountain culture. No one wants to be in the position of telling others what to do. The following are notes from a 1967 meeting to organize a civic improvement program which illustrate the effects of this individualist-harmony ethic:

> The nominating committee had no report to make regarding the position of president and vice-president. The committee chairman fell silent and stared at the floor. It seemed nobody wanted the job or wanted to nominate anybody else. The Reverend Hugh Anderson was there to fill the gap. He was a minister with 18 years experience in community development work, and was unanimously elected president. Harold Mills was made vice-president. Mrs. Eastman was made secretary. Thus, two of the four top positions were filled by nonindigenous persons (one from Indiana, one from New York).
>
> The same problem was encountered with committee chairmen; the biggest fear in these cases was over inability to do the job. Nobody wanted the jobs: "Can't do it." "No time." "Already got too many other jobs." Ab nominated Frederick Bryan for one post. Frederick refused and nominated Ab in return. Ab also declined, saying, "I double un-second it!"
>
> Nominations and elections were all unanimous with one exception. Again Frederick was nominated; he himself nominated Ab. Any contest was precluded by unanimously electing them cochairmen. After the meeting, each tried to get the other to take over the first duties of the office.

The theme of familism in the modern subculture seems to differ in some small degree from its expression in the traditional subculture. Definite allegiance is paid to the family group, and kinship is used for purposes of social identification. There exists also an emotional tie that goes beyond loyalty, which is felt by representatives of both ways of life, a feeling that might be described as rootedness and whose major symptom is dire homesickness when an individual is removed from home for any time. But familism, a strong theme in the modern subculture, is interwoven with other group ties. There are larger groups of which individuals can be members and with which they must divide their allegiance. There are competing goals to familism, such as success and the achievement of wider social standing. There are other means of identifying people, including oneself, than through family ties: occupation, place of residence, educational status—achieved rather than ascribed identification bases. Thus, a man is not only Creech Gilliams' son, he is also and perhaps mainly, a well-to-do contractor.

There are not such great differences in values and attitudes between the sexes in the modern subculture as were found in the traditional. Men and women want much the same things and would employ similar means to achieve them. One way to demonstrate this fact is to ask men and women what they would consider necessities and what they would regard as luxuries. This is a useful method in informal settings as a means of discriminating between informants' peripheral and central values. Although this procedure was not used in Shiloh in any standard fashion, it is my strong impression that families which could be regarded as most traditional would show a great discrepancy in such lists between husband and wife; what she regards as central is frequently regarded by him as peripheral. Kephart noted this over forty years ago when he said that now and then a man may grumble, "'A woman's allers findin' somethin' to do that man can't see no sense in; but, then,' he adds, 'the Lord made women fussy over trifles.' "[55] There appears to me to be much

[55] *Ibid.*, 331.

greater agreement between husbands and wives in the modern subculture concerning what is sensible and what is trifling. Even here, however, there is not always complete agreement. Ernest Phelps, certainly a modernist, admitted that his wife wanted some things that he thought they could do without.

A freer kind of moral code has often been ascribed to the traditional subculture. Field observations tend to corroborate such an assertion, especially with regard to the men, in the areas of sexual behavior, drinking, and activities that in our perspective would be called antisocial (fighting, bootlegging, thievery, and other lawbreaking). Actually, there are two codes: a strict one espoused by the churches and most women, the other just described. In contrast, the moral code of the modern subculture is closer to the puritanical code of the middle class elsewhere. In this code there are strong taboos against adultery, illegitimacy, drinking, gambling, dishonesty, obstreperous behavior, and laziness—or at least there are taboos against allowing such things to become publicly visible. One young man occasionally serves drinks in his home—to outsiders—but he would be disturbed if he thought anyone in the community knew about it. This individual contrasts with the typical young traditionist, who, if he drinks, doesn't care who knows about it; it is quite socially acceptable among his close associates.

Another part of this modern moral code prescribes churchgoing; almost all families that could be considered modern go to church somewhere. They do not, however, have to take their religion as seriously as a traditionist would if he were a steady churchgoer. One need not undergo an intense religious experience, and one need not strain to live right if he joins a church. Thus, this aspect of the code, too, is strict regarding surface (socially visible) behavior, but its grip on the conscience is relaxed. The same young man who enjoys drinks in his home sometimes is a member of a church that strongly proscribes any dealings with alcoholic beverages.

The contemporary subculture is a way of life characterized by dissatisfaction and striving. These are attributes common to what we call middle-class values, wherever they are found. Motivation for achievement, success, the acquisition of money, power, reputation, material goods, and a "higher" style of life could not conceivably be accompanied by serene contentment and guiltless indolence. In this respect, the two subcultures represent a significant polarization: relative contentment and doing without at one end, and discontent and striving at the other.

To describe the atmosphere as one of dissatisfaction or discontent is not to ascribe to it pathological intensity, however. Indeed, this is a normal way of life for millions of people in the world who survive healthily and even thrive on it, and its compensatory rewards have been so well recommended to most of us that we seldom are able to imagine that any other way of life could be enjoyed. Paradoxically, to be satisfied, in the middle-class view, is to be stagnant.

We may gain insight into the overall process of change in Shiloh if we view it as one in which individuals and families emerge from one subculture and find themselves rapidly engulfed in a subculture that is significantly polar to it. The four types of families in the community can obviously be differentiated on the basis of which subculture they participate in and to what extent they do participate. Type I families are on the whole the most committed to the modern way of life. Type IV's are for the most part immersed in the traditional subculture. The two middle types can be differentiated broadly from the extremes at this point in time by their being enmeshed in both the modern and the traditional: they are offspring of a marriage between two ways of life, a marriage whose vows are irrevocable but whose state is not always blissful.

The middle types, the II's and III's, can also be differentiated from each other, according to their type of participation in the two subcultures. In the case of the Type II family, whose initial identifying characteristic was the holding of a full-time blue-collar occupation or the equivalent by the head of household, the traditional subculture has been fairly successfully submerged. There seems to be a primary commitment to modern ways; most of the conflicts between the two will be decided in favor of the new over the old. In the case of Type I families, such differences between the old and the new will rarely arise—they are that far along the road to modernism. In the case of Type III families, on the other hand, conflicts between the traditional and the modern are also likely to arise, but there does not appear to be as clear a pattern of decision in favor of one or the other. Rather, there seems to be a kind of vacillation, a hesitation between the two, which would indicate that, unlike the Type II's, Type III's are either committed to both ways of life or are undecided. In the truest sense, all four types are in transitional states from one cultural configuration in the past to another in the future, but the configurations labeled as traditional and modern have some stability and duration. Speaking in relative terms, then, it may be concluded that the two middle types of families are transitional from a traditionalistic kind of cultural background into a modern kind of present and future. Though both are transitional, the Type II's appear to have made a decision in favor of the modern, the outside, whereas the Type III's seem to be living under two flags, accepting and rejecting parts of both. Both types of families, as well as Types I and IV, face certain problems as a result of their positions with regard to the two subcultures of Shiloh.

V. *Adapting to Modernity*

By this point a fairly clear picture should emerge, a picture of a community rapidly opening into a larger social system, a community whose economic base is shifting from subsistence agriculture, mining, and timbering to mill and factory wagework, a community made up of different social levels, subcultures, and families. The picture, however, will not be complete until the major problems and stresses as they are felt and dealt with by different families in the community have been described, and until some relationships among the phenomena of change and adaptive modes can be formulated.

When one reviews existing theories or studies of social change he is likely to come away with the impression that sociologists concern themselves almost exclusively with large-scale, global, or macrosocial change phenomena. Much social research consists of the marking of historical trends of one sort or another. Much social theory is on the same high level, the most abstract example being the varieties of evolutionary theory. There is, of course, a wide range of abstractness in theories and studies of social change: from the evolution of whole societies to the process of institutionalization of relatively small groups, from the study of cultural trends or societal demographic trends to the study of the life cycle of a family. But for the most part the macrosocial approach to social change concentrates on indexing change and explaining it at a relatively high level of abstraction. Opposed to change as experienced by the demographer looking at census data, there is another approach which concentrates on change as it is experienced by participants in particular situations. The more microsocial approach empirically involves the study of individuals and groups acting and interacting in situations, and it requires frequently that the student understand the meanings and definitions of situations in the minds of participants, where the macrosocial level of study usually abstracts out global "variables" to manipulate at a distance thrice removed from social reality as it is known to interacting participants.

It is probably not necessary to point out that these two levels of study are not incompatible; they are different levels of abstraction from the same reality, and, in fact, they complement each other nicely. Trends such as those regarding communication and the economy in Shiloh act as the stage set or backdrop against which the citizens of the community act out their parts from day to day. The backdrop, the situational conditions, must be known before the performance of the actors makes much sense. But, likewise, some actors must be on the stage or the setting itself has no function or significance.[1]

In short, social change can be studied on at least two levels, which can be categorized as macrosocial and microsocial. What appears as social trends on the macrosocial level—trends such as those taking place in Shiloh—appear on the microsocial level as modifications of situation, as gradual or sudden, problematic or benign situational "crises" (in Thomas' sense)[2] which must be adapted to.

1 The "situational approach," which supplies a major part of the orientation in this chapter, owes its greatest debt to W. I. Thomas. Others, either independently or through Thomas' influence, have utilized a similar kind of microsocial approach, even in the study of large-scale organizations (for a recent example, see Jean H. Thrasher and Harvey L. Smith, "Interactional Contexts of Psychiatric Patients: Social Roles and Organizational Implications," *Psychiatry*, XXVII (Nov. 1964), 389-98. To my knowledge, however, there has been no explicit attempt to link up notions of the situation with the study of social change—though the linkage is implicit in the work of many writers, including Thomas, Parsons, Hughes, and many others.

2 "So long as social life runs smoothly, so long as habits are adjustive, 'situations' can scarcely be said to exist. There is nothing to define when

Two general areas of change emerge as the dominating trends in Shiloh since 1940. One is the changing economy: the closing of some occupations and the opening of others, the increasing need for cash and the decreasing ability of families to sustain themselves through subsistence farming and home manufacture. The second lies in the relatively rapid opening up of the community to the outside world, exposing its members to alternative life styles and values through increased travel, communication, and use of mass media. These two areas of change are not unrelated but are mutually interactive: changes in occupation have brought about changes in life style, and exposure to new values—especially consumer desires—has led in many instances to change of job.[3] Furthermore, concomitant with changes in these two areas have been others; an increase in "scale" (as defined by the Wilsons); an increasing plurality and complexity in the social system as roles (especially occupational) have become more differentiated[4]

---

people behave as anticipated. But when influences appear to disrupt habits, where new stimuli demand attention, when the habitual situation is altered, or when an individual or group is unprepared for an experience, then the phenomenon assumes the aspect of a 'crisis.'" Edmund H. Volkart, "Introduction," in *Social Behavior and Personality,* ed. Edmund H. Volkart (New York: Social Science Research Council, 1951), 12. See also Everett C. Hughes on "critical situations," in his "Institutions," in *Principles of Sociology,* ed. Alfred McClung Lee (New York: Barnes and Noble, 1955), 236: "But situations occur in which the expected does not happen and the unexpected does. Such situations are crises in which—to quote W. I. Thomas—'the attention is aroused and explores the situation with a view to reconstructing modes of activity.' The 'cake of custom' is broken."

[3] "Following education and the development of new commitments and tastes, the economic demands of these (traditional) workers can be expected to increase," says Etzioni summarizing an article by Wilbert E. Moore. See Amatai Etzioni and Eva Etzioni, eds., *Social Change* (New York: Basic Books, 1964), 225, 291-99, for the Moore article.

[4] See Werner J. Cahnman, "Culture, Civilization, and Social Change," *The Sociological Quarterly,* III (April 1962), 93-106. He maintains that an increase in cultural complexity (which he calls civilization) marks one of the most important aspects of social change: "The processes which transform a monocultural into a multicultural system bespeak social change" (98). This point is also expressed by Parsons, Eisenstadt, Smelser, and others as "differentiation."

and as greater vertical differentiation has taken place; and a greater involvement of outside agencies in making decisions that affect the local area—the "Springdale" phenomenon.[5]

These global systemic changes might be characterized in a number of ways, and no single statement will take into consideration all important aspects of change. Nevertheless, there is a striking design in this fabric of change which always seems to move to the foreground of our perception. This design is not the changing economy or occupational structure as such, nor the increasing number of television sets and cars as such, though it is intimately bound up with these and other systemic alternations. The dominating trend, rather, seems to be a kind of *transformation of culture,* a change in total way of life. Yet this is still not an accurate statement, because it implies that all families in the community are simultaneously undergoing this cultural transformation and that all segments of the community are marching in lockstep toward urban industrial "progress." Implications of this kind appear to be the consequence of taking whole communities as units of analysis instead of analyzing them as subunits that are affected differently by global changes and therefore respond differently to them.[6] It is not correct to say, "The

[5] Arthur J. Vidich and Joseph Bensman, *Small Town in Mass Society* (Gloucester, Mass.: Peter Smith, 1958). The "surrender" to mass industrial society has not been as complete in Shiloh as it has in Springdale, to be sure, but the direction of movement is the same. Decisions concerning roads, electricity, telephones, schools, public health services, commercial development, and the like are scarcely affected by local sentiment and are mainly determined by county, regional, state, and federal bodies. A local antipoverty agency was just gearing up for action in 1965; what effects it will have on the area await future assessment.

[6] See Herbert Blumer, "Industrialization and the Traditional Order," *Sociology and Social Research,* XLVIII (Jan. 1964), 129-38, for a convincing statement of this point. He contends that within any traditional society there is likely to be appreciable variation in commitment to the past, and that one is likely to find a mixture of five types of response to industrialization: rejection, toleration of industrialization as a separate disjunctive arrangement, assimilation, use of industrialization to strengthen the traditional order, disintegration of the traditional order.

community is moving from a folk to an urban way of life" (or whatever terms one wishes to use), except at a certain level of analysis. It would be more accurate to say, "Both folk and urban (or whatever) ways of life exist in this community, and an increasing number of individuals and families are moving from the former to the latter." Such a statement reflects differences in subcultural orientations: families may be located more or less completely in one of the subcultures or they may be somewhere between; they may be either moving or stationary. The most prominent design in this complexly woven fabric, then, is the emergence of individuals and families from one subculture into another.

Conceptualizing changes in the social system of Shiloh in this way allows the analyst to place any given family on a line connecting two spheres of existence representing two subcultures. The two spheres represent relatively deep commitment to either the traditional or the modern way of life, and the line represents all the possible points of transition between the two. Although movement along this line is almost uniformly in the direction of the modern, it must nevertheless be allowed that the traditional exerts a gravitational pull of its own, even while families move away from it. These forces exerted by two ways of life represent the loyalties, personal influences, group membership, and exposures to contrasting values that make up the situational conditions of particular families.

In describing the kinds of situations in which families and family members find themselves, I am, in a way, characterizing both the situation itself and the adaptive responses that have been made to the situation or to similar previous situations. That is, one's present situation is in part determined by his responses to past situations. This important point was brought forward in an earlier discussion of subcultures, although the terms of the argument were slightly different. The conclusion reached then was that cultures can be regarded, in part, as adaptive responses to situations, as in the case of the shortened-time perspectives of the lower class. But subcultures are not *only* responses invented for the adaptive purposes of the moment; they are relatively stable over time, are capable of being transmitted more or less intact over generations, and have the power to influence definitions of new situations. If the lower class subculture, for example (there is, of course, no such single entity), were only a response to situation, if it were only a contraculture, then it would change as the situation changes. Instead, there is usually a lag of some kind, as the stability of the subculture acts as inertia: people define new situations in old terms and value old things that may not be viable for survival under new conditions. Thus, only conceptually and never empirically can situations be separated from responses, especially on the level of culture as response.

Nevertheless it will be instructive at times if we proceed as though the situation and the response to it were empirically distinct phenomena. The situational problems of the four types of families can then be described.

Type I. There are certain discrepancies among reference groups in Type I families. It appears that members of these families must frequently ask, "Do I accept and judge myself by local standards or by those I know or think to exist on the outside?" There are immediate pressures from family and friends for a member of a Type I family to define himself in local terms. Likewise, there are contacts with the outside through what is learned in school, through travel, through the mass media, which, by their very contrast with local society, might enhance local identification. One is tempted from many sides to remain a "big fish in a little pond." On the other hand, many of these same sources also pull one's identification in the opposite direction. This fact is especially true of schools, mass media, and personal contacts on the outside, as well as any other agent of influence that tends to define individuals in the context of larger social circles.

Thus, for example, storekeepers are faced with the dilemma of meeting the expectations of personal services on the part of his tradition-oriented customers and running an efficient business as it might be run on the outside. The ambiguity toward tourists and the tourist industry is also related to this discrepancy between local and outside standards. Another symptom of the identification problem is the sensitivity to outsiders' criticisms and stereotypes.

Another example of this kind of discrepancy in reference groups is offered by the case of Craig Bowman, who is uncertain how he should define success for himself. By local standards he is already successful in business, occupies a position of leadership in his church, lives in one of Shiloh's newer homes, and is personally liked and respected by everyone. But occasionally he will see a fraternity brother from college, especially one who has a five-figure annual income as a salesman, and he wonders if he could not have made it that big on the outside himself. He is sure he could have, but, as he says, he will never know: "The worst part about it is not knowing whether *I* could have done it."

Similarly, another young man likes to think of himself as somewhat worldly, civilized enough to hold discourse with intelligent outsiders, to go dining and dancing, and to have a social drink now and then. But he is careful to do these things only during off-hours; even then they are closely guarded secrets in the immediate family. These activities are not highly regarded by local people, including his parents. In the daytime, in the public light, he is the congenial local; in private, in the sanctity of his home, or when he is with outsiders, he is the somewhat snobbish cosmopolitan.

Because of the discrepancy in standards, Craig is uncertain where he fits in the local scheme of things: "The other night I said there were four social classes: the low, the middle, the high, and then me, but I've decided I don't fit anywhere here—Craig, the fat, atheistic storekeeper!"

This man has found a solution in staying in the community, being the big fish, and segmenting his life into two spheres. An alternative that others in his situation have found viable is that of migrating to the outside, where presumably they can live by one set of standards. But costs are incurred by this adaptive maneuver, too, because one leaves behind him the safety and security of the little pond, especially his family of orientation. When he returns home, he must attempt again to leave the outside behind him and live by local standards. Thus, he segments his life, playing to the local reference groups at home and trying to be his more worldly self on the outside. Then, too, it seems that once an individual has enjoyed the experiences that life has to offer on the outside, he is never completely satisfied at home. One finds the kind of feelings of marginality expressed by this Type I man:

> I think the Army was the first big change for a lot of people around here. They got out and saw what things were like in the cities, and they've kind of wanted things like that ever since. People have got turned more toward outside ways. You take a feller like me, for instance, every spring especially I get to wanting to go somewhere else, go to some city. But if I go, quick as I get there I'm wanting to come back to these mountains. Everybody wants to come back to them; they still like the mountain ways. In other words, we're in a dilemma.

Another man was asked if he thought getting outside while in the armed forces changed a person. He said, "I know it does. Seemed like all three of my boys was restless when they got back. Couldn't sit still a minute."

An interview with a Type I 30-year-old migrant to the outside who had returned home for his vacation revealed that he was cognizant of some of the costs of migration:

> *Interviewers*: Have you ever thought of coming back here?
>
> *Informant*: I think about it a lot. The cost of living in Knoxville or any big city is awfully high. But it's more than just the cost of living; I guess once a person is raised up here it's hard to get it out of you. The people are a lot friendlier. People live at a slower pace; there's not all the hustle and bustle of the city.
>
> *Interviewer*: How do you feel about your present work in Knoxville?
>
> *Informant*: It's a good job and its pays well. I get awfully tense at work, though. It's all the minor details that eat on you. I do exercises every morning and they help the tenseness. This week at home I've been running up and down the road and soaking up the sun to get back in shape.

There appear to be three positions one can take with regard to the reference group dilemma, regardless of whether he is a migrant or stays in the community. The first is that he can take his cues entirely from the local group, as sometimes happens even when people move out—some of these outmigrants apparently do not even attempt to adapt to their new situations, but continue to define themselves in terms of past situations at home. Second, he can take his cues from outside reference group. If he does this and chooses also to remain in his home community, he must turn his back on local reference standards and groups either flagrantly or covertly. It appears a little easier to choose this alternative if he moves out of the community and immerses himself in contemporary society. Even in these new situations, he may feel marginal and show the signs of overconformity that often accompany marginal membership in a highly desired group; he may become highly competitive and achievement-oriented, or he may adopt conspicuous consumer patterns: several cars, a boat, a new house, expensive clothes. The third position consists of taking cues from both local and outside groups, the position most likely to be taken insofar as an individual is probably in contact with representatives of both worlds, no matter whether he has stayed home or has migrated to the outside. This position amounts to remaining in the dilemma, which is probably resolved from situation to situation through the individual's segmenting his personality and behavior rather than being permanently solved through commitment to one side or the other. The members of any given Type I family, of course, will probably adopt all three positions over a long period of time, but like the pendulum that swings between the extremes, it seems likely that they will naturally come to rest in the middle of the dilemma.

Although there are some inconsistencies between the local and the wider reference groups and standards to which Type I families are exposed, there are also many points of similarity. The basic value of success is shared between the two, and although some of the finer points of the definitions may be somewhat at odds, the consonance tends to be overriding. The local definition of success carries with it a stress on personal qualities such as honesty, friendliness, and moral behavior, which are not as important as sheer status attributes in outside definitions. The dilemma for Type I's is therefore not so severe as some of those facing other families.

Related to this dilemma of reference groups, but analytically separable from it, is the problem in intergenerational differences that sometimes occurs between parents and grandparents. The problem that Kaplan referred to as "the changing role of the aged" is created partly by the underlying phenomenon of generational differences, for if the younger generation had not changed its outlook and way of life the older persons in the family probably would not feel so strongly that they had been "put on the shelf."[7] A lack of meshing of generational gears creates problems on both sides. For the younger generation, the older family members represent a substantial pull toward an older way of life and thus may constitute part of the reference bind. For the older generation, the younger family members may represent the same kind of pull in the opposite direction, which puts them in a bind between wanting to be progressive yet wanting to hold onto the cherished ways of a lifetime.

In the situation of one Type I family the differences between parental and grandparental generations is played down by means of a sort of compromise between them. The widowed grandfather, who in fact lives in his son's household along with his daughter-in-law and four grandchildren, seldom gives advice and does not make his presence felt in an authoritative way. He spends his days visiting his son's store and chatting with friends who stop there. At home at night, he reads the paper in his own chair, sits back and watches whatever television program the rest have chosen, and retires at his own discretion. He lives his own life, but in a most unobtrustive way. Likewise, the son and his family do not seem to intrude into his father's life. Any differences existing between them are not frequently brought to the surface. In fact, the son and his family orient themselves more toward local than outside reference groups and individuals, so that the older man's expectations of himself are not as inconsistent as they might otherwise be.

In another Type I family situation a clearer gap exists

[7] See Berton H. Kaplan, "Social Change, Adaptive Problems, and Health in a Mountain Community" (unpublished Ph.D. dissertation, University of North Carolina, 1962), 108-11.

between the same two generations, where the grandmother seems less willing to compromise some of her ways and her daughter is more oriented toward outside groups than the son just discussed. The daughter married into a Type I situation, and she and her husband live alone, their only child having died some years ago. The grandmother lives in another part of the community. The adaptive technique used to keep down intergenerational tensions in this case is segregation, where each person more or less keeps out of the other's way. Even here, however, there is an element of compromise, for the daughter conforms behaviorally to her mother's expectations when she is around her.

> *Interviewer*: I wonder if maybe there are differences of outlook and differences of opinion between generations—differences between father and son or mother and daughter.
>
> *Informant:* Yes, that happens, I know from myself. The older people are a lot stricter—I guess they are what you would call "better" people than we are. There are differences between the way my mother and me sees things. This is just one little example, but maybe it will show you what I mean.
>
> My mother don't think it's right to wear Bermuda shorts. When she raised us up we were always fully dressed, and if she'd caught us wearing short shorts like some girls do now she'd have killed us. I don't wear short shorts now, of course, but I do wear Bermudas—and she still says things to me when she sees me wearing them. She'll say, "Well, I *raised* you to be a lady," or something like that.
>
> *Interviewer*: What do you do when you have differences like that? Go ahead anyway?
>
> *Informant*: Yes, just go ahead. But I don't purposely do things around her I know she don't like. I don't wear shorts when I go visit her. Sometimes she'll

> catch me here with them. but I won't go to her house wearing them. You have to—I guess the word is "respect"—people like that. Of course a lot of the new younger generation is more callous, it seems like. I think you have to respect these older people my mother's age.

In a third instance, a Type I man in his twenties noted that there was a considerable gap between his father and his grandfather in a number of ways, and that there was less of a gap between himself and his father. It is instructive to note, however, how this lesser gap closed. This young man feels that one of the biggest differences between his frame of reference and that of his father lies in the issue of risk-taking in business matters. He says his father was always quite conservative and did not like the idea of speculating on land or similar long-range ventures. But he feels he has been able to justify his business outlook to his father through argument, persuasion, and demonstration, and says his father has come around to his way of viewing economic growth. They now act together on most business ventures. Thus, through persuasive justification and acquiescence on the part of a member of the older generation, the gears mesh.

By means of various adaptive mechanisms, then, generational tensions are minimized, and sometimes—but not in all cases—members of the older generations are not made to feel that life has passed them by. When younger families engage in something approximating complete segregation of the older members of the family, then these members can usually turn to others their own age in the community for support, frequently through the medium of the church. If they are not part of any family life and yet find no place in the churches or with peers, their isolated situations may well spell personal disaster.

There are other kinds of situational problems and dilemmas facing members of Type I families which should also be mentioned, though most of them appear to be related in some way or other to the basic reference group dilemma. For example, certain modulated anxieties naturally attend the playing of new roles. Persons living in Shiloh spend a great deal of time playing to local audiences, and most are well practiced in playing roles (such as "good old boy" or "pillar of the church"). They are not (and this includes most Type I's) so well rehearsed in playing nonlocal roles to audiences from outside. There is some self-consciousness about speech habits, educational deficits, and other elements of the Snuffy Smith stereotype. There is sometimes almost too great an effort to let the outsider know that they have kept up with the latest news and the latest controversies on the outside, and that Shiloh, or at least some elements there, are not as isolated as the outsider might think.

Perhaps related to the anxiety of not being able to pull off this new role of man-of-the-world is the occasional concern noted about overextension of resources, especially financial resources. In some cases the concern appears to be the reasonable forethinking of a family that wants to plan ahead carefully. In the cases significant in the present context, however, the concern is about resources that have already been overextended, where money has been borrowed and spent for the acquisition of status props, for investing in children's education, and the like; in short, where there has been too little planning. Situations in which families find themselves deep in debt are not peculiar to Type I's, and, indeed, the reasons for the indebtedness may be basically the same. But at least on the level of Type I families, the debt seems to be the result of a haste to achieve a life style commensurate with their definitions of themselves as modern, middle class, "good livers."

Although Type I families are nearest of any in the community to living completely in the modern plane of existence, they are not quite there yet; rather, they are still closing in on it. Yet there is no doubt in the minds of these family members about the direction in which they wish to move. If they have common situational problems, such problems are outgrowths of a frontal assault and not those of indecision in the field, and still less those of defeat and retreat. These are families that have by and large decided wholeheartedly to try out new scripts and to play new parts against the changed backdrop and setting of the area and the community. They need to practice, and they need to resolve the difficulties of playing to somewhat discrepant audiences. If the description of the distribution of and access to resources of various family types in Shiloh given elsewhere is at all accurate, then these families probably have the kind of personal and secondary resources to pull off a successful assault in the long run.

Type II. There is, in one sense, only a shade of difference between the situations of Type I and Type II family members; in this sense it is only a matter of the degree to which families have committed themselves to a certain way of life, the degree to which they can effectively muster resources in pursuit of these goals, and have emerged into the modern subculture. Type II's are generally newer to the scene than Type I's and are more unfamiliar with the scripts. In fact, in some respects they have not always recognized that they are undergoing a cultural transformation. The Type I's are therefore at an advantage, since they more or less openly repudiate the old-fashioned and the local ways of life; this leaves only one subcultural avenue clearly open to them. The Type II's are not as certain of the direction they want to take, though they are committed at least to certain elements of the modern way. Their occupations are evidence of great involvement in nontraditional patterns, for their jobs require a kind of punctuality, self-discipline, and subordination of personal freedoms from restraint characteristic of modern industrial life. Like the typical situations of Type I families, many Type II wives work outside the home for wages or salaries. The houses, clothes, and cars belonging to Type II families look very much like what one would expect to find among middle-middle and lower-middle class families on the outside, evidence that there is considerable commitment to the value of acquiring material goods and conveniences, rather than a commitment to doing without, which we found characteristic of the traditional way of life. Furthermore, Type II families often attend the modernist churches in Shiloh, just as Type I's invariably do.

It is easy, however, to be carried away by the points of similarity and be tempted to dismiss this whole segment of the community as merely a less affluent copy of Type I's. A closer inspection will reveal that the situation of the typical family of Type II is considerably at variance from that of Type I, that the situation of the former presents more adaptive problems to its members, and that the former has fewer resources with which to deal with its problems. For example, a Type II man may desire the same kind of work as a Type I, but not be able to get it because of limited education. The situation and the solutions to the adaptive problems it poses are complicated by the fact that Type II's have not yet left tradition behind altogether, and that they therefore live between two worlds in a much truer sense than Type I's.

For example, although some Type II's do attend denominational churches, others do not. For those who do not, they can either not attend church, or remain in one of the smaller, more fundamentalist churches of their childhood. In the latter setting (and to a lesser extent in the nonchurch and the modernist church setting), the Type II is thrown into a whole set of highly charged relationships with Types III and IV who are capable of exerting a strong pull back to the traditional. The contents of sermons, hymns, and testimonies, furthermore, are pitched toward the traditional and frequently against the kinds of values that sustain a middle-class sense of virtue and right. Congregations are implored not to use anything worldly as a reference standard, except perhaps in a negative sense; in fact, they should take pride in being looked down upon and feel justified that they are out of step with many of their fellows. As one young Type III said in an impromptu sermon:

> I tell you, children-uh,
> Like it says in this here Scripture-uh,
> That the world-uh,
> Is goin' t' hate you-uh,
> And I want to tell you-uh,
> Children-uh,
> That I'm *proud* they hate me-uh!
> That's what it says and it's the truth-uh.

In playing down the importance of education, material well-being, and popularity and respect among higher-status individuals, the fundamentalist churches serve a definite function in cushioning self-images among low-status groups, but they also raise doubts among those members who have also been exposed to the middle-class gospel. That traditional religion exerts some influence even among persons who have changed memberships to more modernist churches is shown by one man who still, after changing membership, adopts the restrictive behavioral code common to the fundamentalist "Christian" (a term which has a special meaning in the fundamentalist churches, and which is opposed to the "sinner," a person who has not had a conversion experience and has not adopted the restrictive behavioral code—"is not living right," in local terms): "There's a lot of things you have to give up when you get right, even though maybe you don't see no harm in it. Somebody's always patterning after you, and some things just bothers other people for you to do them, even though it don't bother you. I hate for it to bother somebody else, so I'd just as soon not do them." Included in the list of things this man had given up were pitching horseshoes or playing ball on Sundays, fishing on Sundays, and playing cards—even Rook—anytime.

Not only in the realm of religion, but in many other ways the Type II family member is reminded of the proximity of the traditional subculture. Put in terms of reference figures, he is faced daily in his social environment with significant others who represent both worlds. The people he meets at the churches he attends, or the church members who see him whether or not he goes, are but one example. He usually has relatives, many of whom are participants in the traditional way, others of whom are committed to outside ways. Many of his peers in the community with whom he grew up, drank, hunted, fished, and fought are still around to invite him back to a less restrained and more relaxed way of life. The neighborhood he lives in is probably a mixture of Types II, III, and IV, so that tradition is only as far away as the next house. On the other hand, the people he drives to work with, the men he meets at work, his superiors there, all beckon him upward and onward—and most husbands and many wives spend much of their waking hours in an industrialized work setting.

In the area of the family itself, on the surface there appears little difference between the pattern of working wives in Type I and Type II families: many wives in each type work outside the home. Yet there is usually a difference in the formal authority structure and in the attitudes of Type II's about the phenomenon of working wives. The husband is somewhat more the boss of the Type II household, whereas Type I's seem more equalitarian. Equally significant, he is quite sensitive in many cases about this business of changing sex roles. In one unusual case there is a man who takes it all placidly, but this may be because he commutes to work for most of the week in a city thirty-five miles away—he is not home much even on weekends, when he likes to fish or exercise his coon dogs or join his buddies—and authority problems have little meaning when the potential antagonists do not interact. In the more typical case, the Type II man condones his wife's working as an economic necessity, but he still feels that his word should carry final authority. One man whose wife does not work, and who can perhaps therefore afford to express his more traditional sex-role attitudes, shows his keen sensitivity to female domination. His explanation of the phenomenon is also interesting in that it places blame on the men. He is referring to another family in the community in which the wife is seen as too dominating:

> I wouldn't put up with a woman like that. Almost every time they go somewhere, you'll hear her start in on, "Henry, let's go home," "Henry, it's getting late," and so on like that. It kind of ruins the whole thing for everybody, like when you're all trying to sing. Now my wife ain't like that—if *she* acted like that, I'd tell her the next time she'd just have to stay home. One thing with these bossy wives, now, I'll have to say a lot of men have brought it on theirselves by not working and making their women work to pay the bills. I don't mean that all the cases are like that, but some of them are.

It appears that whereas in the Type I family situation the adaptive problems of working wives and changing sex roles have already been worked out fairly satisfactorily in favor of a relatively equalitarian arrangement (only one exception comes to mind of a husband who is hypersensitive on this matter), Type II families have not yet come completely to terms with them. Again, this would appear to be because they have one foot in each subculture, one of which prescribes the more modern arrangement, the other of which prescribes a formal patriarchal system of authority. A man in this situation probably sees neither and both as completely right, and so he allows his wife to work and to exert some authority in the home, but still tends defensively to claim patriarchal rights when playing to nonfamily audiences, or else avoids the issue by spending most of his time away from home. The issue is also sometimes avoided by the fact that marital partners are scheduled for different shifts and thus seldom interact with each other. Both partners are involved in external economic functions and internal housekeeping duties to some extent. These are in the nature of makeshift adaptational solutions to a problem which takes time to work out under any circumstances, but which is made doubly difficult because the family situation involves two inconsistent and competing definitions of the proper marital relationship.

Type II family members, like those of Type I, have the three basic alternatives of being completely modern, completely traditional, or resting in the middle of the dilemma. None has chosen the traditional altogether, even though it may hold some attraction, and yet none has all the skills, background, or knowledge totally to take on the modern. The Type II seems sometimes resentful that others are more fully enmeshed in outside ways than he is, and this resentment, combined with the traditional emphasis on "being as good as anybody," leads to a kind of defensiveness and competitiveness, directed at higher status groups. At the same time, there is sometimes a partial repudiation of those parts of one's past or one's relatives and friends which smack of backwardness. The competitiveness, a trait that has doubtless helped to move families and individuals up the social ladder, runs against the traditional grain and tends to alienate tradition-oriented friends and relatives. This trait is expressed by one young Type II man in the shrubbery business who has pulled himself up from a rather poor environment. The following notes were made after a coon hunt on which this man, four other men and boys, and I went:

> Personally, Royce is extremely boastful. He has the best truck, the best dogs, knows where the most coons are, knows the shrubbery business inside out, etc. There were six of us walking out of the woods tonight at 1:30. Royce had the only decent light. He led the way most of the time, but once got behind three or four of us. "Boys," he said, "I can't stand to walk behind. I just can't do no good thataway." And he pushed through to the lead—which, no doubt is the secret to whatever success he has attained.

Another man who would be classed as Type II, more clearly expresses the ambivalence felt toward higher groups—they are both positive and negative reference groups for him—and the simultaneous rejection of traditional reference figures. This man, Charles Shores, has managed to alienate his brothers and other tradition-oriented acquaintances, and he has also alienated himself from the persons he wants so much to be like—the summer tourists, the members of the nearby intentional community, and other representatives of the outside and the modern. The following are excerpts from field notes:

> His brothers dress in overalls or mining company uniforms. Most wear battered hats or caps. Charles wears gold-rimmed glasses, his hair is slicked down and well-trimmed, he wears a white shirt, black slacks, and black shoes (shined). He wears a pen in his shirt pocket.
>
> Although he claimed not to have time to waste, he

talked this morning for about 45 minutes about nothing of any consequence. But he *thinks* busy-ness. . . .

I asked when I could get together with him to talk about a few things. "Why, I haven't got time to talk like some of these people that sits around the store on nail kegs all day. Course, you could talk to them until the fog sets in and not know no more than when you started. I could give you some information, but I can't take the time to just set around and talk. A man that lives in these parts has to work like I do to get ahead. Find work to do every hour instead of wasting time."

Charles claimed acquaintanceship with many educated members of the adjacent community. On the other hand, he tried to dissociate himself from that class of men who sit on "nail kegs" at the store all day. He was not friendly with the man who was with me, John Henry, and actually ignored him most of the time. (He referred to such men as "grubbers.")

At one point, Charles said mountain people like himself were poor and ignorant. He was explaining that he resented Florida people coming up here and showing their money and education and pushing people around. Later, however, he gave off the impression without saying anything definite, that he had more education and that he was worth more than most around here. (Most people claim his brothers can buy him out easily.)

His alienation is guaranteed from both sides. From his side, he feels he must not associate with people who represent a way of life he has totally rejected—the idle poor, the hunters and fishers, the loafing class, the men who still try to make their living from the land ("grubbers"). And to protect their way of life, these same people must as totally reject him, for to accept him would be to admit that they possess all the undesirable traits Charles claims. This explains part of John Henry's and Jim Shores' vehement disap-

> proval of Charles: "Don't even none of his brothers come by to see him, except to aggravate him." "I can't stand to be around somebody like that." "He's just plain no good." "He's on the bottom of my list."

A Type I man, whom Charles may well look to as a reference figure, ridicules Charles' striving for success: "Have you met Charles Shores? He's been working at the textile plant a long time now, and he really thinks it's great because he can wear a sport shirt to work and not get it dirty. He says to some of his brothers, 'You boys ought to quit grubbing around here and get work at the plant and do gentlemen's work.' Of course, they could buy him out four or five times."

Thus, it is not hard to see that a person runs certain risks in Shiloh when he decides in favor of going modern. First, he is tempted to burn his traditional bridges behind him, so that if he later runs into trouble or changes his mind about the direction he wants to travel in, all he has to go back to is a kind of I-told-you-so or serves-you-right reception. And on the other hand, he stands a chance of not being accepted by those reference groups with which he positively identifies, either because he plays his new roles foolishly from their standpoint or because he has alienated them by his exaggerated defensiveness. Every Type II runs the risk of being left out in the cold, like Charles. Usually, however, the husband and wife in the Type II family see eye to eye on ultimate family goals (mainly middle-class success goals), so that the family can act as a social-psychological cushion.

In summary, when Type II family members are faced with some problematic aspect of their life situation, they usually choose the modern over the traditional response to it. This is because they partake more of the modern than the traditional subculture in their basic values and attitudes. Their attitudes toward work and the job, toward education, and many times toward religion are evidence of this commitment. Insofar as they have emerged into the modern way of life, they share many of the same kinds of problems of assault described as typical of Type I's. They are subject to the discomforts of playing new parts against a recognizably different social background. Yet these Type II's are not completely free of the influence of the traditional subculture, which is frequently made salient to them through significant others in their social environments. Those who manage to free themselves of the influence of tradition must do so by risking alienation from the lifelong friends and relatives who occupy significant places in their life situations. On the other hand, to avoid isolation, they walk a tightrope between the two ways of life and attempt to keep everybody happy by playing highly segmented roles. This role-playing requires a kind of skillful self-manipulation and consciousness of purpose that is not part of the repertoire of many of these people. Thus the situation of the Type II family seems fraught with problems of both assault and indecision.

Type III. At first glance, Type III family situations seem merely to shade off from those of Type II, just as the latter seemed to be the same basic situation as found among Type I's. But again, there appear to be enough differences between the two family types to warrant distinguishing their situational problems. There are similiarities in reference group problems and sometimes in the areas of changing sex roles and religion, but on the whole there is a different flavor of life in the Type III situation, a different approach to the solution of problems; in short, a different type of family. Underlying both the problems and the responses to them are the twin facts that Type III families live between two cultural worlds and that they have not yet made up their minds whether to hold to the old or change to the new.

Not as many Type III wives work outside the home as do Types I and II, although an increasing number hold jobs at factories, work part time as store clerks, and a very few have their own income from picking evergreens. Those who do help with home finances usually do not overstep their traditional bounds and attempt to dictate how it should be spent. This is generally left to the man, as part of his role as patriarch. The significant exception to this pattern is the number of women who keep back part or all their earnings and run their own accounts at the store separately from that of their husbands. Type III men, like many Type II's, are quite ambivalent about women working and are very sensitive about the women's "taking over." These men may have grounds for concern.

Women appear to have great influence—albeit an informal, submerged influence—in setting family goals and in keeping families on the march toward them. This pattern is true even among Type III families, in spite of the fact that superficial observation reveals a picture of straightforward patriarchalism. There appears to be, in fact, a battle of the sexes going on in many Type III families, in which the women are attempting to lead their families toward a more modern way of life and the men try to maintain their families in that relatively effortless state of traditional life which seems natural and adequate. John Henry Sommers said one day: "I guess maybe the women are more dissatisfied than the men. They want to have more. I tell you, that's ruint more around here—women going to work and making money, helping with the payments and such as that. They get to wanting more say in things." The situation is prevented from becoming a true battle because the women usually take pains to avoid totally alienating their men, primarily by acting the traditional submissive role. For example, one couple is considered by many local people (mainly Types II and III men in the neighborhood or in the family) to be the most outstanding case of female dominance in the community, and it cannot be denied that the wife, Lois, does exert a great deal of control over the family. In fact, for her efforts in raising her family to a higher level of living than her friends, neighbors, and relatives (through suggesting to and nagging her husband, Henry), she has won the contempt of many people. She would deny her bossiness, however, and would choose the traditional role of the female if asked which role was more appropriate. The following are notes made after an informal gospel sing at Henry's house:

> Between songs at Henry's tonight I asked what they all thought the woman's place in the family ought to be. Lois spoke up first and said, "According to the Bible they ain't supposed to leave the home, and they're supposed to obey their man. I don't guess they ought to vote, either, but I did this time." Hope said she voted for the first time this last time, but that she didn't think she would any more. John Henry said he thought it was a good thing for women to vote, but that they ought to vote the same way their men did. Henry said he didn't think the Bible meant for men to boss their wives around like it might sound. Lois offered her interpretation concerning the Biblical injunction: "I think it means a man and woman should love one another and come to agreements on things and not just tell one another what do do. The man shouldn't just decide something and then tell his wife and expect her to go along all the time."

It is interesting to note that toward the end of this passage, Lois allows room for a less literal and more modern interpretation of the same scripture with which she at first had automatically responded in defense of the traditional female role. It is also noteworthy that Henry tends to side with her in this public debate, perhaps for the sake of presenting a united family front. But he shows his ambivalence about the existing authority arrangement in a later statement, made with sarcastic humor: "I think the man's still boss around here—but the woman's the superintendent. Yeah, he's just the boss!"

In this *sub rosa* battle of the sexes the women have built up a kind of ideological justification for their subversive (from most males' points of view) activities: they blame the men themselves. Thus, the argument goes, if the men would get out and make something of themselves and take care of their families as they ought to instead of loafing around and hunting and fishing and drinking, the women wouldn't have to go to work.[8] Some of the men accept this argument; others counter it with the claim that the extra money from women working wouldn't be necessary if women didn't want so many things that weren't really necessary—things the men think people could well do without. Both Lois and Hope used this argument. But the argument may rest to some extent on myth rather than fact, since neither of these women could name any families where this was now the case; Hope said she knew of one case like that from the past. It is also noteworthy that neither of the husbands of these two women were particularly poor providers, and it is unlikely that they could have warranted the argument. Yet, the women upheld it.

The real complaint of the women seems to be not that the men don't provide, but that they do not share the same sense of values as their wives. What the women see as inadequate provision is only part of this larger complaint. Thus, Type III wives for the main part are trying to domesticate their husbands, i.e., convert them to a more modern set of aspirations. This domestication takes many forms, only one of which is nagging. The women

[8] One man in the community calls men like this "go-getters": "The saying around here is we have a lot of go-getters. The men take their wives to work in the morning and in the afternoon they go get'er!"

generally take aim at the activities and people they see as dragging their husbands in the wrong (traditional) direction: "That Hope is not entirely satisfied with John Henry's way of life was made clear this evening when she asked if I had seen a newspaper article about a woman suing her husband for divorce because he was spending more time with his dogs than with his family. She laughed and said she thought she'd try that." Worse than hunting or fishing or loafing is the drinking enjoyed by many Type III men. Few go on wild sprees, but many enjoy having "a little sociable drink" whenever they can. The women do not drink (with rare exceptions), and they don't like their men to drink. For example:

> Louise does not like Norman's drinking. Her father and brothers drank considerably, the old man laying out weekends and making a mess of himself. She wants no more of that. Norman himself sees no harm in "drinking along a little bit," and Louise usually puts up with it without complaining very loudly. "She just says a lot of little stuff."
>
> I later asked her which she liked better, fishing season or hunting season. "I like fishing season better, I guess. At least he comes home at night then. I really don't mind him fishing; it's the drinking I don't like."

Outside the nagging, the wife's greatest instrument for domestication of the male is the church. It could not be maintained that a man's "getting right with the Lord" and his "living right" is the same as his being converted to the modern way of life; there are many inconsistencies between the fundamentalist gospel and the demands of middle-class success-seeking. Rather, if a man becomes a Christian (by the local fundamentalist definition), he has become at least stripped of certain loyalties and habits that presumably can be replaced by ones more relevant to success-seeking. In short, becoming a Christian is a good step toward making a man over into what a woman thinks he ought to be.

The men most active in the church are indeed those who are "tamed" by comparison to those who are still "sinners," and many of them, significantly, tend to side with the women in their attitudes toward irresponsible men. "Hope said I should have gone to church with them. (There is a revival this week at Freedom Chapel, one of two usually held every year.) The sermon, she said, was on women who work while their husbands loaf. The preacher 'really laid it on' the men that 'lay around and don't do nothing but fish and hunt and loaf, while they make their wives work to pay the bills.' She said she was really saying 'amen' to that." Henry is another example of a man who has become a solid Christian. But many others around him, while they respect him as a Christian, think he sells out to his wife too readily. Here is John Henry's opinion: "A woman is natured like this. It don't make any difference how good a person you are—you take Henry for instance—a woman is always going to find something to go on about." John Henry said this in the context of the question What would you have to give up to become a Christian? His answer indicates that he would start by giving up obvious things like "laying out of church," drinking, and hunting and fishing on Sundays, but that the list of things would have a way of expanding over time to include everything that the women and the churchmen didn't like.

John Henry's case is a good example of what happens in many Type III family situations, where the wife strives toward emergence into the modern while the husband, at best, tags along reluctantly. In this situation there is a constant tug of war between John Henry and the forces of progress represented by Hope, the church, the children to some extent, and his creditors. There may well be a tug of war within John Henry himself, for he is not so totally committed to the traditional that he sees no value in certain creature comforts and other advantages of progress. Still, he hangs back, unsure. And lined up on his side against the forces for progress are most of his peers, with whom he can daily or weekly escape into the woods and live the uncomplicated life. These are his compatriots in tradition.

The following excerpts from field notes may show the kind of dilemma a Type III man can find himself in when caught between these forces:

> Two preachers are helping with the revival. The two of them have been taking turns about eating with various members of the congregation. Tonight they eat at Hope's.
>
> John Henry is almost frantic. He feels very uncomfortable with one preacher in his home, and two is two too many. He begged me to say for supper tonight of all nights, saying, "I ain't too good at this sort of thing. Come on in here and set down. You can't let me down now." [In this situation I was lined up on the side of tradition.] For one thing, he is afraid they might go to work on him to get right with the Lord, and while he hates not to go along with what somebody else wants of him, he just isn't having any right now. For another thing, he is afraid he will have to go to church tonight, and going to church would knock him out of a coon-hunting date. But Hope is happy.

And again, four nights later:

> Tonight the preacher came by and applied a little more pressure. He asked John Henry if he didn't think it was time to change his ways. In fact, he *told* him it was time. These are the most dangerous ("parlous") times that's ever been. You don't know what might happen to you. So many people are getting killed in cars these days, etc. You don't know which

> day might be your last, so you'd better get right while you can. John Henry told him he knew he was a sinner and he ought to do better, but he felt he couldn't claim to be a Christian knowing that he really wasn't. . . . He and the preacher agreed it was better to be an honest sinner than a hypocritical Christian. John Henry adroitly steered the conversation to other matters.
>
> Afterwards, when the preacher and Hope had gone to the revival, he reflected: "You know, it does make a man feel kindly bad, something like that. But I still think being an honest sinner is better than being a hypocrite, don't you?"

It is obvious that the Type III situation is not only awkward for the males but for the females as well. In some ways, in fact, they have a more difficult set of scripts to balance than the men do, since they must play, to some extent, the modern mother, the traditional wife, and the fundamentalist churchwoman. How does a woman spur the ambitions of her children and at the same time play the submissive, traditional female role to her husband? How can she be a good churchgoer and at the same time strive for emancipation from the past to emerge into the wider world? How does she act toward her husband's friends? They are, after all, his friends, even if they do drag him off to go drinking and spend time away from home when he should be putting water in the house. The problems of the wife and mother in Type III situation thus can be seen as reciprocals of many of those of the husband and father.

The fact that situational problems take place against the backdrop of a larger social setting can be illustrated well in the context of the present discussion of male and female differences in outlook. Although direct proof is lacking, it seems fairly clear that migration out of the community over the past two decades has been selective, in that it has taken younger persons in the population, and more males than females. There has been much speculation that migration has also been selective in removing the more industrious and ambitious from the region.[9] If this is true, it means that unmarried females left in the community have a somewhat limited pool from which to draw their spouses, and must often marry men with relatively low aspiration levels. One Type I husband and his wife made independent observations that many women in Shiloh marry into a lower social level, and a physician in a nearby county theorized that most family problems were caused by this imbalance due to selective migration. Whether this is true or not, it is certainly plausible that the gap between the modern outlook of most women and the traditional outlook of many men, especially in Type III families, is widened by this pattern of migration. My field observations indicate that there exist many families at levels II, III, and IV, in which the wife has more years of education than the husband, indicating that such a gap may indeed exist.

Family roles are also played out against the background of increasing occupational involvement of women in this and other, higher levels in the community. As the assessment of the situation by John Henry given below indicates, greater involvement of women in this external, instrumental function naturally leads to their more direct involvement in decisionmaking processes. It also indicates that this changing pattern affects not only those women and men directly associated with the change through the wife's employment but also a number of nonemployed wives and their husbands.

> I guess there has always been some women that sort of run the family, but I believe this thing of women

[9] For example, Brown and Hillery note that "Appalachian people desiring higher levels of living have had few alternatives to migration." James S. Brown and George A. Hillery, "The Great Migration, 1940–1960." In *The Southern Appalachian Region: A Survey*, ed. Thomas R. Ford (Lexington, University of Kentucky Press, 1962), 54.

> going to work has had something to do with this that you're talking about, don't you? I mean, when a woman goes out and makes money, and maybe the man gets down and can't work for a while and she has to meet payments and stuff like that, I'd think she'd want some say about more things. That'd be natural, don't you think?
>
> Tell you something else about this woman business. I think some of these women that do work has some influence on the ones that don't. Like they might get to talking to one another: "Why don't you do this or that?" or "Why don't you make him quit laying out?" or things like that. You know how they'll do sometimes.

As with other types of families and their adaptive problems, there is a range of solutions with which the participants can meet their problems. With regard to the men, John Henry's response of heading for the woods represents perhaps one of the most frequent patterns. Even he does not totally segregate himself from his family or from other agencies of the modern world, however, and he is somewhat ambivalent about that way of life—he likes parts of it and dislikes others, he is beginning to feel the weight of work and family responsibilities, he says he knows he should think farther into the future about things. Henry, on the other hand, represents a kind of compromise between the traditional and the modern which goes farther toward the latter than John Henry's response. But one should not get the wrong impression here, either, since Henry could by few standards be considered modern: he is marked as being out of the mainstream by his refusal to believe that the world is round, if by nothing else. Most Type III men have compromised with the demands of their situations in some way or other as these two men have. Their compromises are unstable, however, as they are uncertain in many concrete situations which way is right, and they are likely to change as the situation dictates. John Henry, for example, shows a surprising flexibility in adapting to a variety of interpersonal situations. He is not unusual in possessing this talent.[10]

The responses of the women to the problems inherent in their situations have this same twofold quality: they can go either way, toward the traditional or toward the modern, depending on the demands of the situation. It is clearer in their cases, however, that beneath it all they have decided that they and their children are going to find a place under a larger sun than their menfolk are. One might say that whereas the men compromise in order to gain time to live the traditional way a little longer, the women compromise in order more effectively to reach their long-term aspirations for a higher level of living and a fuller participation in a larger social system.

If change "upward" or "downward" occurs, it seems likely that what will determine from which direction the push comes is the economic situation of these families. Largely because of the wife's influence, most Type III families buy on credit, paying monthly for stoves, refrigerators, television sets, pianos, cars, and housing improve-

[10] This apparent flexibility in interpersonal situations is not to be confused with expertise in taking the role of the other or in role playing generally, or what Lerner calls "empathy." There is a difference between being able to play a number of roles in a number of situations and the ability to play the *same* role in a number of situations. As I see it, some Type III men are learning to play the traditional role in a variety of situations, rather than dropping out of those situations entirely as others do. This may be a first step toward learning new roles appropriate for new situations which members of Type II and Type I families already have taken. This is a step that most Type IV's have not taken, for they have effectively left the stage. (Some Type III men would also fit this latter category.) But Type III's generally make only minor modifications in their traditional roles in adapting to new situations, and do not undergo complete role transformations, a skill that seems to require a certain level of knowledge of social reality. The "positive adjustive capacity of human beings" of which Inkeles talks is, after all, a variable, not a constant, and the ability to learn how to adjust to changed surroundings is not equally shared by everyone. Alex Inkeles uses this phrase in his "Social Change and Social Character: The Role of Parental Mediation," in *Social Change*, ed. Amatai Etzioni and Eva Etzioni (New York: Basic Books, 1964), 344.

ments such as running water and indoor sanitary facilities. As Type III families are attracted to the new comfort and status of shiny modern gadgetry, they are becoming enmeshed in an economic system that requires a fairly dependable source of cash income and, thus, steady work habits and other attributes more suited to life in industrialized society. As long as this process of increasing involvement in the economy remains stable, these families will probably move into modernism at a gradual and steady pace. Sudden economic reverses, on the other hand, or other major crises would probably set in motion the more basic traditional response patterns learned early in life, so that the movement of Type III families under these circumstances would be "downward."

The discussion of adaptive problems on the level of Type III families has concentrated on those aspects of the situation which demand inconsistency in the role performances of members. It is realized that other kinds of adaptive problems exist, both for Type III and for the other family types, but it is felt that this reference bind is the problem which is at the same time most central to most family members and most directly related to the change processes occurring in Shiloh. There are other kinds of adaptive problems, among them the problems presented by temporary migration of the husband and the resulting role gap in the family, the problem of deciding whether to remain in the community or gamble on making it better on the outside at the cost of weakening home ties, and the special problems of the very young who daily are faced at school with a way of life that must be reconciled with life outside the classroom. There are also doubtless special problems for the older family member, although it appeared to me that families on the Type III level had not yet begun to nuclearize to the extent of segregating older persons, who were included in households and in family interactions to a much greater extent than in higher level families. If a generational gap exists among Type III's, it exists between children and parents, and even here it tends to be between daughters and fathers, the sons tending to take after their tradition-oriented fathers. But these problems did not seem so great to the participants as those produced by the competing cultural representatives in their situations. Their problems are primarily ones of indecision.

Type IV. Once again, the Type IV families present a somewhat different order of situational problem from those found among other types of families. Unlike Type I families, they are for the most part not committed to the modern way of life; unlike Type II and Type III families, they are not even very undecided; they are committed to the ways of tradition. These are people who have by and large lived the farthest back in the coves and away from the main roads. Their geographic situation is, perhaps not coincidentally, indicative of their social and cultural situation, in that they have lived out of the mainstream of American society and out of the currents of change that have swept through the local community. Their geographic situation is symbolic in another way, too, because change has brought roads, powerlines, and people past many of these once-isolated cabins and shacks, and it has become more difficult for these people to ignore the new ways of life. Thus, the problems of the Type IV family can be characterized as problems of retreat rather than problems of assault or indecision; problems of maintaining a way of life within a system that is established on a set of values contradictory to it, problems of simultaneously insulating oneself from the demands of this larger system which increasingly intrudes itself on one's affairs, while managing to survive within it.

The situation can legitimately be called one of intrusion because, in distinction to Type III's who to some extent go to meet outsiders naturally in the course of their daily rounds of life and work, the members of Type IV families seldom take the initiative in interacting with people who are oriented toward outside ways. Rather, except for occasional trips to the store, the doctor, or the evergreen wholesaler (or perhaps occasional jobs), they stay to themselves by and large, visiting among themselves and going to church and picking galax together as their major forms of social activity.

The intrusion can be illustrated in a number of ways. For example, Type IV families live closer now to roads and highways, not because they have moved toward them, but because the roads have grown out to reach them. They are nearer to telephones for the same reason. And for the same reason they are nearer to neighbors who live on a somewhat higher level and who are more involved in the modern subculture, so that the visibility of alternative ways of thinking and living is higher. Likewise, when outlanders from Florida and other areas come to the mountains to search out summer havens, they look for the remote, Waldenesque settings such as Type IV families now inhabit, and more times than not they settle within shouting distance from some such family, so that, again, the visibility of outside ways is increased and the insulation of the purely traditional is broken. The expressed attitude of these summer residents might be called one of peaceful coexistence, but it is hardly one of respect. One man who plans to live in Shiloh about five months out of the year said: "There's one thing you can say about these local people: they just aren't interesting people. You have exhausted all possible conversation in about twenty minutes. They are mostly honest, sometimes hardworking, but they are living a vegetable existence." This man wants to find somebody in Shiloh who is conversant in his field of international relations. Another summer resident from

Florida says he wants to preserve the backwardness of the area, because that is what attracted him to it.

> He thinks there are a lot of interesting characters among the local people. He does not seem anxious to convert them to anything, even though he does not understand them and feels they are backward. He feels that many of them are either content with or resigned to their situations.
>
> "Some of these families have an electric range but no running water. Now, how much trouble would it be for Guy Patrick to put in running water? And off the back porch there is a dirt path; whenever it rains it turns into a mud puddle. He could put a rock in it to walk over, but he'd rather walk through it or around it."

It is difficult to tell to what extent these latent reformists' attitudes get across to the families in question, but it is unlikely that the message is completely lost. Furthermore, the attitudes of some of these summer residents are not so latent. The man who is quoted at length below lives in a settlement of Floridians across the ridge from Shiloh, where a colony of some two hundred outlanders have moved in. His statements reveal not only his perception of traditional values but also the ways in which the summer residents (together with a somewhat progressive-minded wife) impinged on the life of one man obviously rooted in traditional ways.

> You take this fellow down the hill here. His wife was pretty sick, but she still walked two hundred yards for the water for him to drink and wash his face in. He kept an ancient privy I guess thirty yards away. As other people here and in town got these (new conveniences), the men had to make concessions. This man finally grudgingly got water running to a basin on the back porch. Later he grudgingly ran it

> into the house, but he refused to put a faucet on it because he said he couldn't stand the thought of drinking stagnant water that had been standing in a pipe. So the water ran through the floor twenty-four hours a day. This year, he's finally conceded and put a faucet on the pipe. He hasn't changed his philosophy, but *he's been forced by circumstances to change the way he lives.*

In answer to a question as to what the respondent thought these circumstances were, he replied:

> The circumstances? Well, his wife, who works at the school cafeteria now and *sees the way things are done, and being around others who have these things.* In other words, progress has caught up with him.
>
> His wife talked him into buying asbestos siding for the house. He did finally get the siding, but it has laid around in his yard for three years before he has gotten around to putting any of it up. Somebody asked him why he didn't put a bathroom in the house. You know what he said? He said, "You think I'd put one of those stinking things in my house?" Finally, after about five years, he put one in, but you can't convince him it doesn't stink.

The respondent is referring to a man who from this description would probably be classified currently as a Type III rather than a Type IV. This outlander's feelings about local persons who are even more rooted in the traditional subculture might be even more intense.

It is true that tourists and summer residents have some influence on *all* types of families in Shiloh. They have contact with the local entrepreneurs, who are mostly from Type I families, in their initial entry into the community and in church and social activities after they have settled there. Their influence on that level is in providing role models from outside the region for persons who wish to become assimilated into middle-class American society. On the other hand, they have considerable contact with Type IV families, who are their neighbors, and whom they hire to work for them at odd jobs. For some Type IV's these outsiders may be role models, but for the majority they are only reminders of what they themselves are not and do not especially want to be—in short, negative reference figures. As the last informant noted: "These local people are perceptive, very perceptive. People who come up here and 'put on a show' are not accepted. I guess you could say there is a resentment of what they think is an unnecessary display of money and education." He feels that outsiders provide positive role models for the young and the better educated: "The young, the educated people see us and see that the outside is different from what they have known. They see that the old people just don't have it. Outsiders are coming in and changing the philosophy." But, he should have added, this is not so in the cases of most Type IV's, where even he noticed resentment.

The negative reference function of most outsiders and city people in general is implied in the note made on a Type IV man to the effect that he didn't want to eat where "town people" politely "picked around at their food" instead of digging into it. This man's brother expressed the same kind of reaction to "big" churches: "I just don't feel right in one of them big churches." Likewise, many Type IV's express resentment of outsiders who move in and inhibit the accustomed freedom of movement by posting their land. One older woman gave the following expression of resentment of certain people who come in and show off their city ways; she was asked, "What do you think about all these Florida people coming in these parts?"

> If they was all like this Barnham, I wouldn't like it. He's the hatefullest, spitefullest man. He come into

> the store one day while I was there, looking for somebody to do some work for him. He asked about this one boy. "Will he work?" he says, and they told him they *reckoned* he would, and he said, "But I mean will he *work*?" and on and on like that. Then he's fenced off his land and put up signs saying, "Don't Put Your Foot on This Land."
>
> There's others that are real nice, and I wouldn't mind them coming in here at all. This one that said he had a lot of cherries this year and had done picked all he wanted, and he said we were welcome to pick some as long as we didn't hurt the trees—which you can understand. He was real neighborly.

In short, outsiders are really only acceptable if they meet the expectations of the local traditional subculture. As Collier says of the people of the depressed areas of Stirling County, "It is you who must sacrifice a part of your values to reach equality with them—and if you can do this, they will be your friends.[11]

It is not only tourists and summer residents who are bringing elements of contemporary outside society to the doorsteps of Type IV families, though they provide a clear example. Also noteworthy in this connection are the agents of programs conceived outside the region which are aimed in one way or another at upgrading living conditions and changing attitudes. In addition to the county department of public welfare, agencies of both the federal and state wars on poverty were active in Shiloh during the summer the fieldwork was conducted, and their activities were directed at many of the families classified here as Type IV. It was too soon to tell what the impacts of these skirmishes were, but attitudes toward the war on poverty in general were mixed, regardless of level of the community.

It is easy to romanticize the traditional subculture, but

[11] John Collier, Jr., quoted in Charles C. Hughes and others, *People of Cove and Woodlot* (New York: Basic Books, 1960), 246.

it is also easy to see it only as a negative response to life conditions and to the dominant, middle-class subculture. As Miller writes in an article on the lower classes, "A good deal of the tone of discussions of the 'lower class,' even by sociologists, has a negative quality. On the other hand, a few seem to have a romantic feeling about the 'lower class,' . . . and see them as rebels against the horrors of middle-class, conformist America."[12] It is difficult to be objective when discussing cultures and subcultures; perhaps one should only attempt to point out what he sees as the positive and negative functions of a subculture for the participants in it.

Certainly it could not be claimed that the traditional subculture is the perfect solution to the life situation of Type IV families and that problems only occur because of the interference of middle-class people from outside it. Even if the participants were completely isolated from modernity, there still would be the problems that seem to accompany poverty everywhere. Chief among these is finding a way to make a living or a way to supply the necessities for physical survival. There are problems of illness, family crises of various sorts, problems of unplanned parenthood (including illegitimacy), housing, diet, and transportation, to name but a few. Furthermore, it is plausible that shortened-time perspectives and the devaluation of the success motive, as well as other aspects of the traditional subculture have played a positive role in that this negative outlook has prevented disappointments and has allowed for adaptations that a less relaxed set of standards would not have permitted. It has also presented a kind of cushion in its stress on familism and the importance of personal relationships, for persons who could not find social supports in any other system (people who would have failed for one reason or another to achieve

[12] S. M. Miller, "The American Lower Classes: A Typological Approach," *Social Research,* XXXI (Spring 1964), 1-22.

success as defined in another system). As Gans writes, "The responses which make up a subculture are compounded out of what people have retained of parental, that is, traditional responses . . . and the innovations they have developed in their own encounters with opportunity and deprivation."[13]

It is true that once a cultural response like this is born, as with any culture, value, or adaptation, it has a life of its own, and an inertia, which means that individuals born into its midst will have it transmitted to them regardless of their capacity to make it in a different system. This has happened among Type IV's in Shiloh, where generation after generation of bearers of tradition are being created, while at the same time the requirements for adaptation are themselves changing. There is a kind of cultural lag of which some observers of contemporary Appalachia write in terms like those of Pearsall concerning the neighborhood she studied: "Little Smoky Ridge stands as a twentieth century illustration of the persistence of a frontier type of social organization and value system in an environment no longer suited to either."[14] Even more simply, as Merton quotes Kenneth Burke, "people may be unfitted by being fit in an unfit fitness."[15] But if one wants to find blame or cause for the unfitness, the lag, or the maladaptation, he can find it either in the inertia of the culture or the disturbance from outside or inside the system which has changed the conditions of life; neither by itself is a sufficient cause. Two objects are required before one of them can be out of phase.

Certain problems would have remained, even if the modern way of life had not intruded upon these people.

[13] Herbert J. Gans, *The Urban Villagers* (Glencoe, Ill.: Free Press, 1962), 249.

[14] Marion Pearsall, *Little Smoky Ridge: The Natural History of a Southern Appalachian Neighborhood* (University: University of Alabama Press, 1959), 42.

[15] Robert K. Merton, *Social Theory and Social Structure* (Glencoe, Ill.: Free Press, 1957), 198.

But since the intrusion has happened and is happening, it is changing the requirements and definition of successful survival and therefore has raised the problem of adaptation to an entirely different plane. For if one takes seriously the messages sent by the ambassadors from modernism, not only must he cope more vigorously with the problems he has been coping with for generations, but he must also give up the adaptive tools he has used to cope with them, since those tools—elements of the traditional—are themselves seen as part of the objectionable problem. Not only has the terrain changed, but the guide map is being taken away. It seems to me, then, that the major adaptive problem confronting most Type IV families is not illegitimacy or personal pathology or joblessness by themselves, but that of preserving a culture and a mode of adaptation being withdrawn slowly from them. The response to this threat could naturally be expected to be in a traditional vein; it amounts to a withdrawal, a retreat, an attempt to insulate oneself from an alternate way of life clamoring for attention on all sides.

Yet it is not so simple as it sounds, for the reason that one can live on an island and be unaware of the surrounding water for only so long, and for the reason that these families still must survive, and they must do it in the context provided by the larger social system. As Clarence Haskell said, "'Bout the only thing that worries me is keeping out of debt. Seems like it's so easy to get in debt any more, and you can't never get out." He spends the money he gets "mostly paying bills and paying debts. Mostly car payments." To quote again what he said on a later occasion, "Feller has to work *oncet* in a while. Enough to keep the bill collectors away." This minimal-work outlook is probably the most pervasive one among Type IV men, although there are some who say they would like to have steady jobs. Johnson found among men whose families were receiving Aid to Families with

Dependent Children (ADC) and Unemployed Parents in Kentucky that 85.5 percent say they have looked for work. One wonders how seriously they sought work, however, when "the method of seeking work most often indicated was that of asking friends and relatives."[16] The writer is reminded of Howard, Clarence Haskell's brother, who announced one day, with the wistfulness of a man who dreams of the possible but improbable, "I'd like to get me a job"; or of Clarence himself, the intensity of whose motivation for work is indicated by these notes made one morning when he found it too wet to pick galax.

> Clarence said to his son, Lester, "Let's go over to Maggie and see about some work clearing brush for them Florida people." Lester said he thought he'd go work on a car engine he had extracted the other day. Clarence and I talked some more. Pretty soon he got up and went out to where Lester was tinkering. He sat down in the grass. "Let's go over to Maggie and see about some work." Sonny (a young boy who had arrived earlier) suggested we pitch horseshoes instead. Clarence said a man had to work once in a while, the galax wasn't any good.
>
> About that time Bill Rivers drove down in his pick-up, parked beside the road, and got out and sat in the grass. "What you'uns doing?" Clarence said, "We're thinking about going over to Maggie and see about some work clearing some brush."
>
> A few minutes later, Clarence said, "Let's go on over there. I got 75¢ here to buy gas with; that ort to get us there." Clifford (another boy who had by that time joined the group) asked why we didn't go up and pitch some horseshoes. Clarence said, "We better go on over." He got in his car and Lester put down

[16] Cyrus M. Johnson, "Mountain Families in Poverty" (unpublished paper, Departments of Sociology and Rural Sociology, University of Kentucky, Social Research Service and the Agricultural Experiment Station Cooperating, May 1965), 17.

> his cleaning rag and got in with him. They drove off down the road. . . .
>
> By this time it was 9:30. All this had taken nearly an hour and a half. Later in the day I learned that neither had found any work that day.

The object is not so much to find work as it to find a "means," to which work is but one avenue. (The word *means* is used here as in the sentence, "This is a nice place to live if a person just has the means.") Another means besides employment for wages (which rates low because work requires regularity in attendance and because one is working for someone he may not know or especially like) and galacking (which rates high in popularity because it is outdoors, is unsupervised, and can be engaged in more or less spontaneously) is that of the agency check. The agency check, whether from welfare, Social Security, Army retirement, Unemployment Compensation, or some other source, probably constitutes a *sine qua non* for many of these families, although precise data would be difficult to obtain. At least one informant, Guy Patrick, when I asked him how he was able to make it nowadays, admitted, "We wouldn't be able to make it at all if it wasn't for the help we get from the welfare."

Even with the agency check, families of this type must deal with representatives of the modern; the applying for funds itself means that Type IV's must secure their survival by coping in a way acceptable to the agencies holding the purse strings. Thus the agency, like the world of work, provides a context within which these people must cope with their needs.

The school is another aspect of the Type IV situation, for the school is a great window to the outside and the contemporary. For Type I's, the educational system is a means to consolidating status gains and moving on to greater accomplishments, and for Type II's and many

Type III's (especially the women) it is a place to send your children so that they can have something better than you have. For Type I's a college education usually is assumed. For Type II's a high school education is hoped for, and for Type III's a high school education is not so likely as completion of the eighth or ninth grade. But for most Type IV's, education is something for other people; type IV's usually have few hopes for their children getting as far as high school. The children of these families may not do as well in school as other children (this is one of the premises of Project Headstart, at any rate). It is almost a certainty that they feel self-conscious about their appearances, especially in consolidated schools where there are enough pupils from different levels of the community to form a miniature copy of the community stratification system. One young lady frankly admitted that she did not like school after she started attending the ninth grade at the consolidated high school. People there were different, she said, and she just never could get used to it.

But mainly, the parents do not seem to see the relevance of a formal education for the probable future circumstances of their children (if they see the future at all). They have heard that it is important and they sense the truth and meaning of the advertised correlation between education and income, and in fact many are able to pronounce the value of education in glowing terms just like everyone else; or not quite like everyone else, because one wonders if they really believe what they are saying. There is a parallel here to the attitudes toward work just described.

> Carl Patrick wants to see his children get through high school and would like for them to go on to college, although he is very doubtful that the family can afford the latter and he was not . . . insistent on the former in view of the increasing costs of sending them to

> school. He himself went to the seventh grade, as did his brothers. He recognizes the need for a high school education in order to get good employment. He expressed no regret that he did not have such a background, though he did seem preoccupied with fancied ways of making money and getting jobs. He is somewhat ambivalent about education, as he states that he "learned more in the Army about getting along—just common sense—than I learned all the time I was going to school," and that "experience is the best teacher."

Some parents reject "too much education" outright because it is "misused," and "brings harm." The schools and education are rejected on religious grounds because "There's too much science taught," "It leads people away from the Lord," and "There's too much worldly foolishness." (Some also object to the Boy Scouts because it is a "worldly" organization.)

Nevertheless, the children are under the jurisdiction of the school for at least several years, so that the school does constitute part of the total family situation. The children's response to the school varies between apathy and acceptance, the difference apparently hinging on how well they are doing at the moment and what alternatives are available to them. Different from pure apathy is an expression of hatred or resentment of school which is sometimes shown. Recent dropouts particularly seemed to center their reasons for quitting school around the resentment of certain teachers. The alternative to apathetic or resentful withdrawal from the school and what it represents is willful involvement in it, and some Type IV children do take the school's messages seriously. What happens when these children return home after school then becomes a problem, both for the children, who must compare what should be with what is and will be, and for the parents, whose own children are now lining up with the other representatives from the outside world, thereby becoming intruders in their own homes. This problem of intergenerational differences can be expected to become a greater one if programs like Project Headstart succeed in their aims, although at the present it does not seem to be too serious.

The Type IV situation, then, is one of attempted withdrawal from a social system in which such families are increasingly becoming enmeshed. Some of the avenues of withdrawal are retreat into the family and the neighborhood. For the men there is also the traditional retreat into the woods. Last, one may retreat into one's self or into alcohol. None of these solutions is completely satisfactory, for all of them provide semipermeable membranes through which the outside way of life can seep. Some of them incur even higher costs than the original problems themselves; at best, most are temporary coping devices and not long-term adaptive solutions.

VI. *Success or Failure?*

Because of the increased national interest in Appalachia as an area of concern, it is of some importance to ask how well the families of Shiloh have coped with their problems. Are these people without hope, resigned to whatever fate decrees, dissatisfied with their lots but unable to find solutions to be worked toward? Or are they, on the other hand, adapting to their situations in a constructive way, sizing up their problems, and searching for solutions to them? Are there differences between family types in the degree to which adaptive problems have been met successfully? These questions are more than just academic ones, since their answers have implications for the problem-solvers interested in Appalachia and the millions of people who are affected by their programs. Before they can be answered, however, we need to look more closely at the notion of adaptation itself, and the difficulties associated with evaluating adaptive success and failure.

Adaptation is commonly conceived of as a process in which a person or an organism or a system of some sort adjusts to a crisis or problem that he or it faces. Sometimes the process of adjusting leads to a more favorable situation for the thing doing the adjusting; sometimes it leads to a less favorable situation. The term *adaptation* refers only to the process itself and not to the outcome. We usually think of this process of adaptation as being influenced mainly by one thing: the crisis or problem itself. It is true that adaptation is initially triggered only by some disturbance in the environment, but once set into motion, it is clear that other factors also come into play which influence the course of the adaptive process. The bulk of these other factors fall into a category that we might term *resources,* defined here as any source relied on for possible solution to adaptive problems. These resources may be of several orders. They may be personal resources, such as native problem-solving ability or amount of influence over the environment. They may be social resources, such as those provided by membership in families, friendship groups, or businesses, or linkages to financial or educational institutions—all of which might be called upon for help in coping with various problems. Or they may be cultural resources, which all of us use when we automatically turn to the customary way of doing things.

An individual's resources may equip him well to meet the problems at hand, or they may be deficient in some way. Furthermore, individuals vary with regard to their access to resources of various kinds, the values that they place on their use, and their knowledge of how to use them. A shopful of tools is of no avail in building a house if a man doesn't know a saw from a hammer.

Thus, not only does the magnitude of the problem affect the course and outcome of adaptation, but so do the quality and availability of resources for coping. To understand adaptation in Shiloh requires some knowledge of resources as well as familiarity with life situational problems. Understanding the nature of adaptation in the abstract is no great problem, since the basic idea has been around for some time. Evaluating the degree of success with which some particular group has met a problem, however, raises more critical questions. The major difficulty is that of excluding cultural bias from the evaluation.

Adaptive success and failure must be regarded as situationally specific. That is, one must take into account the conditions that are being adapted to and recognize that different conditions require and permit different forms of adaptation. Every individual and group has to make it in his or its own ecological matrix. Examples from obviously different cultures would make this point clearly: the average American boy learns that the square on the hypotenuse of a right-angled triangle is equal to the sum of the squares on the other two sides, but he cannot catch a seal, whereas the average Eskimo boy is in the reverse position, as Bierstedt points out.[1] Yet we cannot say that the Eskimo is poorly adapted, nor the American, because each requires different equipment for survival. Not only cross-cultural examples, but subcultural examples as well, make it clear that one must first know the contingencies for survival before he can judge a man poorly equipped. As Honigmann asks, regarding use of the concept of stress in social psychiatry: "Doesn't the nature of psychological stress make it much more likely that to know it requires understanding the situation the distressed person confronts, how he interprets the situation, and what compensation he receives? Especially when the social psychiatrist deals with a culture in many ways different from his own does it seem important to hold firm to a phenomenological point of view in identifying psychological stress."[2] His question applies equally to the concept of adaptive success.

Clearly, as Honigmann points out, no definition and no objective measure of maladaptation can be without bias, or rather, without being stated from the point of view of some value. One must always ask about adaptation, "Adaptive by what standard?" The best one can do, it

[1] Robert Bierstedt, *The Social Order* (New York: McGraw-Hill, 1963), 127.

[2] John J. Honigmann, "The Middle-Class View of Poverty Culture, Sociocultural Disintegration, and Mental Health," presented at the University of Kentucky Centennial Conference on Cross-Culture Psychiatry and Psychoethnology: Culture Change, Mental Health, and Poverty, Aug. 1965, p. 17.

would seem, is to make explicit some adaptive standard and stick with it, remaining aware that he has taken a value stand, thereby minimizing his bias.[3]

Two indicators of adaptive success and failure occur to me as being potentially less culturally biased than others one might choose. These are the level of satisfaction or dissatisfaction expressed by the persons adapting, and the physical and mental health status of these persons. There are, of course, problems associated with the use of expressed satisfaction as an indicator—how do you tell when a person is distorting, repressing, or exaggerating, for example—but these seem to be technical problems of measurement rather than problems of underlying bias. Using health as an indicator also involves technical difficulties, since factors other than the strain of adaptive failure influence disease processes, but one might assume that these factors are relatively constant from population to population, so that comparisons of rates are meaningful. Although neither is completely free of bias, they are certainly less biased than some other indicators of disorganization that one might use, such as the extent of broken homes, crime and delinquency rates, or number of families on welfare. The latter, paradoxically, could be used to measure *successful* adaptation in certain circumstances. Fatherless homes may, for instance, be the most workable solution to the problems of the urban lower-class Negro, given the facts of low employability of Negro males and the requirements of the ADC program. High migration rates are sometimes used to indicate disorganization and social pathology, but it is obvious that migration may be the best solution to the adaptive problems of many groups.

There seems to be some advantage in measuring adap-

[3] The writer is indebted to Edwin H. Rhyne, College of William and Mary, for the distinction between being unbiased and being "value-free." He maintains it must be possible to be "objective" and still hold some value.

tive success and failure by letting the individual be his own judge, although this is not usually done. For some reason, social scientists and social engineers usually import their own middle-class and professional criteria into settings that are foreign to them, and invariably they conclude that the picture is black.

There is a different kind of justification for using health status as an indicator. The underlying assumption is that the model of stress and adaptation which is found in much of the thinking of medical scientists (such as Hans Selye) can be adapted to the "life situational approach" taken in this research. One who holds this position, for example, would agree with Patrick, who says, with reference to his study of modernization among the Papago Indians, that "insofar as . . . stresses are not cushioned by small group systems . . . they may be expected to 'spill over' into personality and somatic disorders."[4]

It is fairly clear that success in coping is associated with family type. There are two reasons for this association. One is that the number and magnitude of adaptive problems are disproportionately distributed among the various families, the other is that adaptive resources are also unequally distributed among the families.

Some problems are shared by all families: everyone needs more money, everyone suffers the normal recurrent crises of family life—death, birth, separation, illness, and accident. But such problems are more numerous and more intense on the lower end of the scale of types, and new and different problems appear toward this end of the occupational scale. Although Types I and II may worry about where the money is coming from, this is not the same as being anxious for one's food and shelter, as some IV's are. When illness strikes in a I household, it is

[4] Ralph Patrick, "The Modernization Process Among the Papago Indians," paper presented at the 63d annual meeting of the American Anthropological Association, Detroit, Nov. 1964.

unfortunate and inconvenient; when it occurs in a IV household, it is a calamity. To such worries as these must be added the threat of gradual erosion of one's way of life, which is sometimes the case among families near the bottom of the scale, and the normative confusion felt by those who are not yet fully modernized.

Type I family members stand between two sets of reference figures: those from the outside and those from the local area. Norms received by Type I's from these two sources are not always consistent, though there is a strong base of support in the home community among family and same-level friends, which helps minimize conflict. Type II family members, although they have for the most part made decisions in favor of higher-level local and outside reference groups and standards, still have strong ties to relatives, friends, neighbors, and churches who exemplify a more traditional way of life. Generally speaking, however, even here the family acts as a safety zone of sorts, since all members tend to strive for consolidated goals of betting life. Among many Type III's the decision regarding reference standards and figures has yet to be made, particularly among the men, who are attracted to some of the material and life-style aspects of the modern way of life, and who are at the same time attracted strongly to more traditional ways of earning a living and enjoying the present whenever possible. The women in such families are often trapped between their men and their desires for betterment, which are fanned by other women who are working, have migrated out, or have married into more fortunate positions. The men, on the other hand, feel the pressure from their women, joined sometimes by the church and their children, to "live right" and take the first steps toward a well-disciplined modern life. But they also feel "the call of the wild," as it were: the call of lifelong friends, male relatives, and traditional culture heroes, real and fictional. The Type III family itself is pulled apart by its divergent goals, and there is often no comfort for the confused, undecided member.

Type IV families are another story again, their reference standards being as traditional as is possible in an era of blaring television, brash tourists, screaming jets, and wars on poverty. Mixed with the traditional is the so-called culture of poverty,[5] and it is difficult to tell where one begins and the other leaves off—which is positive value and which is only a response to deprivation. Whatever the source or the reason for maintaining this culture, most Type IV family members cling to it and yet cannot entirely escape from the contemporary culture; they must survive within the environment set for them by the larger social system. Thus, they, too, are caught in their own kind of reference dilemma.

Not only are problems more severe, but resources for coping seem less adequate among persons at the lower end of the occupational scale. The traditional mountain culture has been likened to a "frontier culture," in that it is adapted to a stationary condition—it is not geared for change or for adaptation to new conditions. Therefore the persons who are socialized into it are not prepared for change either, and they lack the kinds of cultural tools —the thoughtways, habits of looking ahead, the constant circumspection and vigilance for changes in the very conditions of existence—which are the keys to survival in middle-class, industrial society. As Dubos has said, "The state of adaptedness to the world of today may be incompatible with survival in the world of tomorrow."[6] They have little talent for scanning all possible alternative solutions to a problem and rationally selecting the one best suited for a long range, optimal outcome.

[5] See Oscar Lewis, *Five Families* (New York: Science Editions, 1962), 2-3.

[6] Rene Dubos, *Man Adapting* (New Haven: Yale University Press, 1965), 271.

There is that knack for making do, which is exercised to the hilt. Several tradition-oriented men in Shiloh, for example, buy the cheapest car imaginable, figuring that a person doesn't need any better, as long as it runs most or part of the time. Then they buy a second "old trap" like the first, except it doesn't run; it is used as parts for the first. When the car quits running after several months, two other cripples are bought, and the original set is left to rust in peace beside the road. Indeed, I found I could roughly index the subcultural orientations of neighborhoods by the number of junked cars beside the road. As it is with the automobile, so it is with the rest of life. An "old trap" will get us by.

Occupations, like cars, have a way of running down. The story in agriculture and mining has already been made plain. But a crucial incident occurred during the summer of 1965 which shows the difference between the traditional and the modern response to change: the mica operation in Shiloh shut down. What were the responses of the eighteen or twenty men who were left without work? At first, the layoff was regarded as temporary; in fact, this was a belief supported by the manager of the company. Every man signed up for unemployment compensation. Some who had side interests took advantage of the extra time to clean fields, tend shrubs, do some trading, fix up houses, and the like. Some of these men started looking for work that would be steadier; some of them eventually took jobs in nearby mills and factories. Others among them did nothing in the way of economic activity right away, but took advantage of the time off to camp out and go fishing and make regular beer runs to Jenny's (a bootlegger near another community) and to the next county. One of these men eventually made a little money by bootlegging himself, but found it too much work and too little profit. When the layoff dragged on over several weeks, three of these men made a tentative plunge into the world of industry. They sought and obtained employment in a mill one day, went to work for part of a week, and then decided they had better things to do. At the end of the summer they were still unemployed. A third category of men who wanted employment and were conscientious workers were also still unemployed at the end of the summer. They wanted to work, but they knew only mining, and perhaps a few related skills, and they were unwilling—they felt they were *unable* —to go into another line of work. Also, they were unwilling to travel long distances each day to get to work—they did not want to leave home. One day I overheard two men who fit this category conversing in front of a store. James Haskell is a brother to Howard and Clarence Haskell; he is the oldest of the Haskell brothers, and he has worked steadily for Northern Mica Company for years. Ollis Vance, like James, would be considered a Type III. "James is thinking remotely of other work possibilities. He and Ollis talked this morning about what a good business was being done in shrubbery by every man who had gone into it. But, James said, it is awful worrisome to start off on simething new like that." Ollis likewise seriously contemplated moving into work in the furniture industry, but by summer's end he had still not convinced himself this was what he wanted to do. He and James and the others who remained unemployed would just make do until the jig and the grinding plant opened up again. They did make out somehow, and seven weeks after the temporary layoff, the operation began again. The men's faith in mica was repaid. But in November I received word that the operation had shut down yet again, and the word was that it may be closed for good this time.

Jack Snyder expressed his view of the problem in this way: "I'll tell you what one big trouble with the workers around here is—they've just learned to do one thing, and when that one thing goes out, they can't seem to do anything."

In Linton's terms, Types III and IV are members of a "folk culture" in which "the core constitutes almost the whole."[7] Unlike the culture shared by Types I and II, the traditional subculture has few of the elements Linton would call Alternatives, which represent "different reactions to the same situations or different techniques for achieving the same ends."[8] In Linton's thinking, a certain number of Alternatives are necessary for successful cultural adaptation; they are new ideas and techniques that are tested in changing circumstances.

Thus, "making do" and "getting by" have limited utility in securing longrun adaptation. The traditional personality has neither the goals nor the means for achieving goals that are the optimal survival requirements for an industrial, middle-class-dominated setting. The personality of the modernist is much better suited to this environment because he is more flexible and future-oriented. His goals of economic and prestige success are well-suited for survival, as is his ability to take the role of others and present himself differently in different circumstances. Somewhere in his life, the modernist has learned how to profit from experience, how to look for change and adjust to it and even take advantage of it. He has learned how to adapt.

The modernist has learned to subvert or suppress certain goals in order to achieve others, and the resulting rank-order is more suited to contemporary life in the mainstream of America than is that of the traditional man.

[7] Ralph Linton, *The Study of Man* (New York: Appleton-Century-Crofts, 1936), 283. The core culture is constituted of universals, "those ideas, habits, and conditioned emotional responses which are common to all sane, adult members of the society." (See *ibid.*, 271-87.)

[8] *Ibid.*, 283.

Thus, for example, freedom from restraint and authority is valued by both, but it is not worth much economic sacrifice to the modernist. To the traditionalist, on the other hand, economic considerations are secondary. For instance, "I was told a tale of a man named Gordon who got mad at Eldon Steele, then new at Northern Mica as superintendent. He'd been working in Africa or somewhere, used to bossing people around and telling them what to do in a way that just couldn't go over here with these people. Finally, he told Gordon he'd done a sloppy job on something he was supposed to have done. And I mean he didn't do it in a nice way; he just told him what a lousy job he had done. Gordon just said, 'I quit.' Then he punched Eldon Steele in the nose. I guess he'd have killed him if they hadn't pulled him off. He really did a job on him."

Educational considerations are also secondary to the traditionalist. Take, for example, the case of these two dropouts:

> The other day Harve (John Henry's brother) was telling me why he quit school in the tenth or eleventh grade. "This boy was looking off my paper and I just had it up where he could see it. That old teacher come back there and took my paper and told me I got an F on the test. She never done *nothing* to that other boy. I never went back there again." Another of John Henry's brothers says he quit school in the ninth grade because he didn't like the English teacher. This is something besides just projection. It is impatience and impulsiveness which is seldom curbed (at least in boys) in these families.

Stories like these could be multiplied. But the stories are almost always about tradition-oriented III's and IV's; I's and II's are sympathetic but are rarely directly involved in such incidents.

The observation above concerning "impulsiveness which is seldom curbed" was inserted in the field notes on the strength of the patterns of child-rearing which I have seen. Most boys in the community, except for those of Type I families, were given a great deal of freedom. Discipline was inconsistent, spontaneous, and hardly ever effective in terms of controlling behavior. Male children were referred to as "mean boys" by their parents, half-approvingly and in the presence of the children. Differences in socialization of the young may help to explain differences in adult personality. It may be due to the benefit of hindsight, or ad hoc reasoning, but the consistencies between childhood and adulthood appear striking to me. The following notes refer to a Type I family; it would seem incongruous to hear a Type III or a Type IV complain of his son like this:

> I asked my boy to clean out the store bathrooms the other day. He mopped around the outside of the commode a little bit and messed around some. I went in there later and the trash can hadn't been emptied nor the floor swept. He said, "You didn't tell me to empty the trash can."
>
> Then I told him to sweep off the front out here, and he went out and pushed a little dirt down the walk here—there was more trash to be swept on out to the road than there was close up to the store here. He said I didn't tell him how far to sweep.
>
> Same thing with my girl and washing dishes: "You didn't tell me to dry them."

This is a significant lesson in learning responsibility and initiative. Not all parents here would care that much about how the job was done, if done at all.

A similar kind of personality difference shows up in early adulthood: young men reared in tradition-oriented households seem to remain in adolescence far beyond their teen years. Contrast the following excerpts which show the attitudes toward marriage of a Type III and a Type I man.

> Amos has just bought a '58 Ford convertible from his brother, and today the transmission "tore up, I mean tore up." He flagged me down at Sally's station and asked if I would ride him out to Harry Cooper's to pick up an old transmission from the latter's '51 Ford. Harry and two other boys were performing surgery on Amos' car in the rain, shirtless. On the way out to the Holler, Amos asked what I was doing here. One thing led to another, and soon he was talking about marriage.
>
> "Boy, I don't like being married. No, sir. She wants me to stay home all the time, and I don't like staying around the house. I *don't* (stay around the house) either. She never says much; she might carry on a little bit sometimes. When I stay out pretty late sometimes she says some little old something, but if I get mad she shuts up. I might come in late and been drinking and get mad and then she don't say nothing. She waits till I get sober!"
>
> Amos has been married eight months.

On the other hand:

> "Marriage changes you, psychologically more than physically. Before I got married I didn't have to think much about what I was doing and what I was going to do. Especially before Crosby (the informant's toddler son) came along, I know I never thought of a man building a home before he was well set up and about thirty-five years old. But I'm in debt over my head! Yeah, I think marriage and children make you think about the future more; they give you responsibilities."

These responses to marriage represent more than just responses to marriage; they are symptomatic of an underlying tendency to respond to all things in a certain way, whether it be education, work, or any number of adaptive problems. Insofar as all families in Shiloh must live to some extent in a social system that sets "contemporary" standards for survival, we must tentatively conclude that tradition-oriented families inappropriately socialize their children, especially the males, and that, therefore, adult personality often has resources inadequate and inappropriate for optimal survival on the terms of that system. This is not to say that no tradition-oriented person ever makes it satisfactorily. On the contrary, many members of Types III and IV families lead satisfying and healthy lives. But the risks to happy survival and adequate adaptation are raised by deficiencies in socialization such as those described.

When the social system of the family is considered as a potential adaptive resource, it will also be seen that there are variations in the kinds of resources offered by different family types and the effectiveness with which they can meet the problems confronting members.

The family's function in the socialization of children is clear: it is one of the chief mediators between culture and neophyte members of society. The family as a social system has an important role in shaping the personalities of its members.[9] In other words, the systems from which resources may be drawn are linked to each other, so that personality, family, and culture can be kept distinct only conceptually. The family as a social system, for example, may be described on a continuum that runs from complete involvement in the larger social systems of neighborhood

[9] See, for example, Jacob W. Getzels and Philip W. Jackson, "Family Environment and Cognitive Style: A Study of the Sources of Highly Intelligent and of Highly Creative Adolescents," *American Sociological Review,* XXVI (June 1961), 351-59. Their findings on creativity parallel observations made by Claudia Lewis on the lack of creativity in rural mountain children in her *Children of the Cumberland* (New York: Columbia University Press, 1946), which she attributes primarily to home environment.

and community (and area, region, state, country) to isolation from them. Lidz has pointed out the potential consequences of socialization of children in families that bear deviant family cultures.[10] The linkages between personality, family, and society in Shiloh become clearer when it is recalled that the farther down the scale of family types, and hence the more traditional the family, the more likely the family is to be self-contained (or of low scale) within its neighborhood or itself, and therefore the more likely it is to be deviant from the surrounding contemporary social system in the culture that it supports.

The family can offer several functions to members besides that of socialization; chief among them is the satisfaction of physical and emotional needs. The meeting of physical wants is most easily accomplished where there is greater economic solvency (command over money, food, and other goods), so that, clearly, the adequacy of this kind of support is closely related to family type. Actually, even among families that do not command much economic power, there is a willingness to share and a strong cultural pattern reinforcing the sharing and borrowing of whatever a family member has, so that even on the levels of Types III and IV families, a little goes a long way. Family members on these levels can help one another survive, but they cannot very easily help one another progress as those on higher levels can. As a Type I who had migrated to the outside said about the difficulties facing the "little man" who might want to go into business: "You need a lot of capital to compete these days, and if you don't have banking behind you, you can't get anywhere. The little man, well, when you are trying to hold down a job and raising a family, working five days a

[10] Theodore Lidz and Stephen Fleck, "Schizophrenia, Human Integration, and the Role of the Family," in *The Etiology of Schizophrenia*, ed. Don D. Jackson (New York: Basic Books, 1960), 339.

week and trying to keep in groceries, medical expenses, clothes, car payments, house payments, and things like that, you can't get ahead." If one has neither the financial resources nor the family behind him, getting ahead or even maintaining the status quo is that much more difficult.

Aside from the family's potential as an economic resource, it can be an important resource for the gratification of emotional needs for members. The theme of familism is a strong thread running through the whole fabric of Shiloh. But there are also variations in the basic theme from one family type to another. Familism, which is frequently expressed as "closeness" in Shiloh, is not the same as the togetherness that many of us have assumed to be the ideal family arrangement. Not all families in Shiloh plan activities together, arrange schedules so that all members are at home at certain times, or even eat together regularly. Familism is instead psychological, a tie that need not be given constant expression in overt symbolic action. Thus, one may feel emotionally supported by his family even when it is more characterized by apartness than togetherness.

Nevertheless, the more overt form or expression of family cohesion may make a difference in the degree of support a member feels he gets from his family. It is one thing to feel a tie to home and hearth, and another to go home and find it empty. It is one thing to feel that your family is behind you in a pinch, and quite another to feel that it might be better not to go home tonight to avoid being nagged. Thus, the tensions described between men and women, especially in families of Types III and IV, present an obstacle to the giving and receiving of full emotional support, and these families may more frequently be handicapped in their function of providing a cushion for members' adaptive problems. Families of Type I, and perhaps those of Type II, are probably on the whole better able to provide this kind of resource, as they tend to be more overtly cohesive.

Other social systems can, of course, offer both aid and comfort, i.e., both economic and social support. For that matter, other social systems besides the family can be important in socializing and helping to form personalities. The school is an important potential resource in the last regard. Indeed, families of Type I, and increasingly the other family types, do make use of educational resources in resolving dilemmas of adaptation. But families most steeped in the traditional subculture have neither the cultural values nor the personal inclination for the most part to use this resource. In fact, their using the schools would only serve to heighten their dilemma; doubtless this happens sometimes, though there is no data on it at present.

Except for their relating to agencies such as the county department of public welfare and an occasional contact with shrubbery wholesalers, Type IV families do not make use of secondary resources. Type I families, at the other extreme, make much fuller use of banking, insurance, governmental agencies, and other kinds of agencies that would be classified as secondary.

Resources other than the family for emotional support or the cushioning of adaptive problems are, especially for members of families of Types III and IV, the peer group (for men) and the church (for women and some men). Supportive functions for family members higher on the scale may be played by the church or by mass media (such as written fiction, movies, and television serials).

With regard to resources, it must be tentatively concluded that members of Type IV families probably have the weakest personal, familial, and cultural resources for dealing with most adaptive problems, with Type III families running a close second and Type I families at the other extreme with the strongest resources. One of the key resources, found on the personal (or cultural) level, is the ability to adapt itself, and the inability of Type IV's and many Type III's to deal with adaptive problems as adaptive problems, and to meet them with long-range optimal solutions, is their major resource weakness.

From this knowledge of differences in problems and resources one would expect to find more signs of adaptive failure at the lower end of the scale of occupational types. My impression is that this expectation would be borne out if expressed dissatisfaction and ill health were used as indicators of failure. Regarding dissatisfaction, it is significant that even when a number of III's and IV's said they were satisfied, they added the qualification that, "a feller has to be, don't he?" This is more akin to resignation than satisfaction.

Despite the feeling that differences in adaptive success and failure exist among these four groups in the community, another strong impression must also be recorded. I left the field with the general feeling that despite the existence of some cases of obviously malfunctioning individuals and families in Shiloh, the dominant tone of life is one of widespread satisfactory adaptive outcomes for most of the citizens. I share along with Honigmann and Mead the view that social scientists "listen for distortion with both ears," ignoring the plain fact that most people manage to see the situation through in one way or another.[11] Indeed, the present study has concentrated on adaptive problems and disruptions, weak resources, and consequent pathologies, to the partial exclusion of consideration of the circumstances of untroubled situations and good resources and adaptive outcomes. And, indeed, most of the people of Shiloh are healthy and satisfied most

[11] John J. Honigmann, "The Middle-Class View of Poverty Culture," 5.

of the time, and their families for the most part remain intact. "Things change so gradually," said Mrs. Greene, "it happens so slow you don't pay any attention to it. It just happens." She could only speak for herself, but, she said, "It don't bother me anyway." I think she spoke for most of Shiloh.

VII. *Observations*

Certain things are obvious from this study. One is the fact of change in Shiloh and, by implication, in the many other Shilohs throughout Appalachia. Change is occurring on several levels and in many areas. The striking changes documented in some areas lead one strongly to suspect change in less easily documented areas such as the realm of attitudes and values. Differentiation in the occupational structure and status differentiation in the community in general are outstanding features of the recent history of Shiloh. Changes in these economic and social structural areas, I suspect, are intimately connected with increased acculturation into the wider society of the United States—more specifically, the dominant society of the urban middle class. Encompassing and partially explaining this trend in differentiation is the trend toward contact with the larger society, both through greater volume of communication and through the reaching-in of industrial interests from the outside. All these changes are part of the package that some social scientists have loosely called *modernization;* they are characteristic of social changes taking place in many other parts of the world.

To an economist, the term *modernization* means something like economic expansion, or *industrialization.* To a political scientist, it means something like changes in the political structure in the direction of constitutionalism, *democratization,* and wider political participation. To some social scientists, the term is interchangeable with *westernization,* an equally amorphous concept indicating changes in political, economic, familial, and other social structures, in addition to changes in attitudes, values, and customs. Modernization may also connote *urbanization, rationalization, secularization,* and *differentiation.* Last, scholars like Lerner and Inkeles suggest that modernization has to do with personality characteristics or states of mind such as empathy and "readiness for new experience and . . . openness to innovation and change," which seem more psychological than sociological phenomena. It seems helpful to regard the type of changes to which modernization refers as *changes in cultural values and orientations;* concepts like industrialization, urbanization, westernization, and so on are thus left to describe other specific, essentially noncultural, varieties of patterned change, whether structural or psychological.

A further problem with the concept of modernization is that while its referent is supposed to be a universal process of social and cultural change, attempts to find and identify the universal aspects of the process have been frustrated. It seems that we are dealing with a classical kind of conceptual problem which Simmel dealt with more or less successfully in the last century: the problem of form versus content. Where Simmel insisted that a distinction should be made between forms and content of social organization, it would seem that in the case of modernization a distinction should be made between the general form of this type of sociocultural change and particular contents that are local, regional, or societal expressions of this form. It is suggested that a useful general definition of modernization as a form of change would be that form of cultural change which is interpreted by participants in a social system as a movement *from* an orientation toward traditional thoughtways *toward* what is regarded as more contemporary, less archaic ways of thinking. The particular values and orientations that are regarded by participants in the social system as "older" and "newer" comprise the specific *content* of the general form of modernization. Thus, a man in India and a man in the Appalachian United States may both be undergoing modernization, but the particular values being left behind and the new values being adopted are probably quite different in the two settings. The only other way in which we can find "universals" in modernization, it seems to me, is to look for them on the level of personality change, as Lerner and Inkeles do.

Obviously, by the meanings just given the concept in the preceding paragraph, there is a strong dimension of modernization in Shiloh: there are segments of the community accepting and rejecting "old" and "new" cultural orientations with varying degrees; and there has been a movement of families along this traditional-modern dimension over the past decades.

Some interesting and potentially instructive parallels and divergences are apparent when this portrait of Shiloh is hung beside some other recent studies of change and modernization: certain Eskimo community studies, Lerner's description of change in Middle East countries, Benvenuti's research in a Dutch farming village, and Gallaher's restudy of Plainville. In Berreman's description of culture contact and change in the Eskimo village of Nikolski, for example, it is said that today it would be "a pretty funny fellow that didn't depend in part for his livelihood upon wages and canned food purchased at the store, and that didn't use mail-order furniture and clothes, listen to the radio, and send his children out to high school."[1] Still, part of the traditional way of life remains despite the heavy overlay of white mainland culture. Significant, Berreman feels, is the fact that although villagers have accepted the white man's goals, there is little hope of achieving them in the village, a situation that he feels has

[1] Gerald D. Berreman, "Inquiry into Community Integration in an Aleutian Village," *American Anthropologist*, LVII (Feb. 1955), 55.

led to dissatisfaction, interpersonal conflict, and depopulation. This is not so much the case in Shiloh, where there are more resources for dealing with changed circumstances and more means for achieving new goals, so that many of those who wish to remain in the community can make it if they so desire. Employment in nearby factories and the development of tourist services offer perhaps the most important new means for achieving the new goals in Shiloh.

Although Berreman generalizes when he says that the white man's goals have been adopted, he does report that there is a group of outside-oriented villagers and a group of traditional village-oriented people,[2] indicating that there is some of the same two-worlds flavor to life in Nikolski, and presumably the consequent reference binds that seem to be characteristic of Shiloh.

Chance describes an Eskimo village that has experienced culture change with quite different results from Nikolski.[3] In the case of Kaktovik, Chance feels that because culture contact with whites was accompanied by employment opportunities, the newly acculturated goals were achieved and no significant community disintegration was experienced. He further found that all families were equally able to participate in the new way of life, and that there was no resulting conflict between the new and the old, such as exists in Shiloh.

A third example from Eskimo community studies shows that cultural change in a St. Lawrence village has involved a shift to new standards whereby the mainland has become a dominant "reference culture" for the Islanders.[4] With the exception of noting that younger people identify with the mainland culture more quickly than older people,

[2] *Ibid.*, 56.

[3] Norman A. Chance, "Culture Change and Integration: An Eskimo Example," *American Anthropologist*, LXII (Dec. 1960), 1028-44.

[4] Charles C. Hughes, "The Patterning of Recent Cultural Change in a Siberian Eskimo Village," *Journal of Social Issues*, XIV (1958), 25-35.

Hughes does not draw attention to differences among reference standards within the community, but presumably such differences do exist.

In all three cases of Eskimo communities, the coming of cultural change, particularly new or outside attitudes and desires, is linked to participation in a rational, nontraditional economic and occupational system, a relationship that I have tried to underscore in the case of Shiloh. The need for cash is a central factor in the early phases of the shift from tradition to modernity. When a family shifts from a subsistence economy to a money economy, it has flipped the switch, so to speak, of a new system of life that gradually ingests them. Economics, of course, are not alone at work in social change, but it certainly appears to be a prime mover in Shiloh.

In contrast to this idea is Lerner's theory that the progression from tradition to modernity begins with urbanization and extends through literacy and media participation to empathy (the ability to play alternative roles and take the roles of others).[5] Lerner sees media participation as the *determining* factor in industrialization and economic participation: "rising media participation tends to raise participation in all sectors of the social system."[6] This point of view comes close to being a new brand of single-factor determinism. In Shiloh at least, increased media participation is only one of several factors at work producing modernization, and it is not absolutely clear that media participation is an independent rather than a dependent or simply concomitant variable.

Lerner does present an interesting typology of personality types (or social types?) based on his researches into modernization in the Middle East: the traditional, the transitional (with three subtypes), and the modern,

[5] Daniel Lerner, *The Passing of Traditional Society* (Glencoe, Ill.: Free Press, 1964), 61-63.

[6] *Ibid.*, 62.

which parallel closely the family types described for Shiloh.[7] Lerner finds the basic differences among these types to be psychological rather than social, but, significantly, the personal traits Lerner ascribes to his types (such as constrictive selves, self-manipulation, empathy) are somewhat similar to the subcultural traits that I have ascribed to the Shiloh types.[8]

Benvenuti's study of Winterwijk, a Dutch farm community, utilizes neither the concept of modernization nor empathy as such, nor the role of mass media as Lerner's work does, but it is similar to Lerner's study of the Middle East in many other ways.[9] Benvenuti contrasts farming attitudes and practices, styles of life, and family patterns through the construction of a scale and a typology similar both to Lerner's and my own. The scale, which is referred to simply as "the score," roughly indexes Lerner's "empathy."[10] "The score" is related positively to socioeconomic status, to modernity of farm management, to neighborhood relatedness, to nuclear family patterns. There is an inverse relation between "the score" and distance from paved roads. Types of farmers and their families, according to Benvenuti, range between the very progressive and the very conservative; his descriptions of these two ideal types closely parallel descriptions of our Shiloh Type I's and Type IV's.[11]

The changes that Gallaher describes in Plainville from 1940 to 1955 bear a remarkable resemblance to those occurring in Shiloh: "the steady disappearance of geographical and cultural isolation; pressure for change from the larger culture surrounding Plainville, involving at some points actual interference; the acceptance of new living

[7] *Ibid.*, 71-73.

[8] Lerner's examples from Turkey are perhaps the clearest instances of similarity to Shiloh. See especially 131-35, 153-66.

[9] B. Benvenuti, *Farming in Cultural Change* (Assen: Van Gorcum, 1962).

[10] *Ibid.*, 88-89.

[11] *Ibid.*, 158-63.

standards focused on material comfort and increased efficiency."[12] Gallaher refers to the general change process as urbanization rather than modernization. Again, mass media are found to play an important role in change.[13] Significantly, Gallaher finds in Plainville the same basic economic change as exists in Shiloh: a "long-term shift in emphasis from self-sufficiency to a cash economy."[14] He finds concomitant changes in the prestige system and in relationships between neighbors and kin which roughly parallel my observations of Shiloh. With some modifications, Plainville could pass for a Southern Appalachian community, as, indeed, could any of the examples of modernizing social systems just described.

An interesting exception to the pattern of modernization suggested by these studies is the case of Cantel, described by Manning Nash.[15] Cantel, an Indian community in the highlands of Guatamala, apparently has become industrialized without becoming modernized to any significant degree. Nash compares factory employees to persons engaged in traditional occupations and finds few appreciable differences in family structure, world view, and a number of other areas. His findings lead him to conclude that traditionism has "learned how to coexist with a factory regime."[16] He remarks that "we have come to think of industrialization as the beginning of a drastic chain of social and cultural change which may some day transform the peasants and primitives of the world into one gray mass of proletarians and level their distinctive and valuable ways of life into one or another pale copy of Western life."[17] The case of Cantel shows that this belief is not

[12] Art Gallaher, Jr., *Plainville Fifteen Years Later* (New York: Columbia University Press, 1961), 226.

[13] *Ibid.*, 228.

[14] *Ibid.*, 229.

[15] Manning Nash, *Machine Age Maya: The Industrialization of a Guatemalan Community* (Chicago: University of Chicago Press, 1967).

[16] *Ibid.*, 1.

[17] *Ibid.*

necessarily warranted, leaving us with the unanswered question: Under what conditions will changes in economic structure lead to modernization of culture and under what conditions will it not?

It is clear from these few illustrations that students of modernization, urbanization, and industrialization stand to profit greatly from the comparison of cases of contemporary social change studied in different settings. Such comparative study would reveal which, if any, processes and sequences of modernization are universal and which are accidents of immediate circumstance. Comparison might also highlight structural features that facilitate and interfere with modernization processes. It would be helpful, furthermore, in guiding refinements of the concept of modernization itself, which in its present usages means many things to many people and is really not a single process at all. Comparison of the Eskimo studies especially underscores the utility of comparative study in understanding the consequences of change for different types of communities and for different types of individuals and families within communities. The present research on a changing community in Southern Appalachia provides yet another case to be used in the comparative study of the elements and consequences of modernization.

The present study takes seriously Blumer's contention that a single society can show multiple responses to the introduction of industrialism.[18] I have attempted to show how global changes can sweep through a small community and yet not touch all parts equally. I have carried Blumer's idea further by applying it not only to the societal but also to the community, family, and individual level; for example, how a variety of families faced with problems will respond differently to them.

[18] Herbert Blumer, "Industrialization and the Traditional Order," *Sociology and Social Research,* XLVIII (Jan. 1964), 129-38.

Most writers on Appalachia have perceived, subliminally at least, the dual quality of life there. It may be more than dual; in fact, I am sure that such subcultural duality is cut across by a rural-urban dimension and a subregional variable beyond our immediate scope. Not only is there a traditional way of life here, but a modern way of life as well. The latter is not in all respects like middle-class America elsewhere, but it is quite similar. It is important to regard these polarized entities as subcultures and not as people, because many people do not fit into one category or another but are somewhere between, participating in both to varying degrees. The transitional mountain people comprise a large proportion of the population, and they, like the other types, are faced with their own problems. Particularly of those most recent converts from traditionalism it might be said that they are faced with the most challenging problem life can pose: how to play the game of survival when the rules are changing.

The moderns, though much like their middle-class city counterparts, are not yet quite the same, especially in their own eyes, and herein lies a fact of some importance. Not only in the display of stronger family ties and a remaining core of other soft-pedaled traditional mountain qualities such as individualism and person-orientation, but also in the conception of self as a mountain person one finds points of distinction between the mountain modern and the outland modern. This self-concept is perhaps most evident in the attempts to play it down—through joking, overcompensation, and so on. Occasionally, the defensiveness is expressed more directly. This self-concept is rooted in a culture that creates in a man a sense of identification with geography, topography, natural ecology, and fellow mountain dwellers.

Reflecting on the life situations of the four family types that were constructed primarily on the basis of occupational type, it becomes apparent that there are some problems all face in common. The most pervasive one verbalized is that of making a living. In addition, there are family crises of a natural and recurrent kind, such as death, separation, and illness, which families at all levels must cope with. There is a difference in the quantity and intensity of such problems among these families—the IV's face more and deeper problems than the III's, and so on to the I's. But also important is the existence of problems of different orders at the various levels. There is a hypersensitivity about being mountain-bred among the I's; there is a double standard of sorts, local versus outside, which can lead to dissatisfaction and confusion among such relatively well-off families. Some of this same concern exists among II's, in addition to mustering extra resources for investment in modernism and to concern about relinquishing old ways. Among III's there is confusion about which way is better, about what parts of both can be obtained and reconciled, and about how to resolve the choices offered by friends, relatives, and acquaintances who are unwitting representatives of two subcultures. Last, the IV's are troubled uniquely by the incursions of outland values on a cherished way of life: how is it possible to keep the alien visitor satisfied and yet maintain the right way of life, to keep his visits from creating permanent inroads?

Styles of adaptation to these varied problems also differ from one type of family to another. Influenced by the subcultures from which adaptive tools are drawn, as well as by the life situation itself, these styles may be described as ones of assault, indecision, and retreat, for the I's and II's, III's, and IV's, respectively.

What can be said, in the final analysis, about the level of success with which the families of Shiloh have met their problems? Has their coping with the problems of change netted success or failure? It is necessary to offer two considerations before suggesting an answer to this important question.

First, it has become obvious to me that one is prone to impose subculturally biased standards of success and failure where they are inappropriate, even in spite of years of training in professional objectivity and detachment. The problem is to arrive at a "culture-free" definition of adaptation. Two indicators that may be less biased than others are the level of expressed satisfaction or dissatisfaction and status of health.

Second, adaptive outcomes are not only a function of the magnitude (if it can be measured) of problems but of the availability and ability to make use of resources in combating problems. Jink Ray, of Kentucky, was able to halt the harbingers of the bulldozer revolution at his property line, while Al Capp's Pansy Yokum (as of this writing) is unable to stop the tides of change. In Shiloh, Craig Bowman can look out for himself; who could say this of any of the Type IV's? Thus, success or failure in coping is a product of both the size of the problem and resource adequacy.

In terms of health and expressed feelings of satisfaction, there is an apparent relationship between family type and adaptive success. Part of this relationship may be explained by the drift of the incapacitated into less steady and less skilled occupations, and part may be explained by the opposite tendency of fit individuals to "float" to better, steadier, more highly skilled jobs. But I do not think all the cases can be explained this way. It is too clear that being a Type IV entails problems and provides few personal, social, and cultural resources with which to combat them, resulting in ill health and dissatisfaction, which in turn become problems in a depressing and apparently endless spiral.

On the other hand, although I think this relationship between family type and adaptive success exists, I am also impressed with the level of success with which the community as a whole seems to have responded to the problems of change. It is not a defeated, hopeless community, but a vital, living piece of social tissue, most of whose families are making it in one way or another. My impression of Shiloh thus contrasts with diagnoses rendered of many other Appalachian communities as sick and dying little places infected by some epidemic virus blown in on the winds of change. Perhaps the next significant study of the Appalachian region will go beyond describing its deep-rooted pathologies and will reveal, more adequately than I have here, how and why some of its people and some of its communities have successfully conquered the challenges of a changing environment. That study is long overdue.

Appendix A
Some Unanswered Questions

Every study probably raises more questions than it answers. Several important problems unanswered by research in Shiloh are discussed in this appendix.

1. Within each family type-level, some individuals and families make it and others do not. There are obviously distinguishable subtypes within each level. What are their characteristics? How is failure to make it related to downward mobility? Is there a discriminable difference in resource availability and usage between these two kinds of families? There are no answers to these questions yet.

2. Another kind of question is related to history of the community. Where did these kinds of families come from? Have representatives of these four types been in Shiloh throughout its history? Or have some new conditions and contingencies of survival created new categories of families? The tentative answer to the last question seems to be yes: Type II's do appear to be a new breed of mountaineer, a hybrid growing where the seeds of modernity have taken root in the soil of tradition. But historical proof is lacking. Also missing is adequate knowledge of the points at which "conversion" to modernity takes place. Are there certain roles in traditional society which place their occupants in positions of greater exposure and less immunity to contemporary outside culture than others? Are there critical periods of vulnerability with regard to age? What we need are more complete case histories of Type II families, emphasizing their patterns of mobility.

A tentative hypothesis is that the changeover from one

subculture to the other occurs as part of a chain of events which proceeds roughly in the following sequence:

1. New consumption tastes are cultivated through a number of influences, leading to acceptance of the values of "living better" and "having more," and also to the actual acquisition of more material goods, usually on credit.
2. Paying off debts then becomes a major concern. If one has year-in, year-out payments to keep up, then he is disposed to look for the kind of job that will provide a steadier income than traditional jobs usually do.
3. The new job (usually factory or millwork) leads to new situations of contact with the outside world, with "rational" and impersonal bureaucracy, with co-workers and foremen who display more contemporary life styles and outlooks.
4. Old life patterns and thoughtways—including friendship and kinship ties and religious beliefs—are found inconsistent with the new approach to life and work. Some old patterns are syncretized with the new; others gradually disappear.

If this chain of events occurs in reality, then a simple formula for engineering change is apparent: give the traditionalist television, consolidated schooling, a Sears Roebuck catalog, and easy credit. Then build a factory within an hour or two commuting distance.

The problem with this simple formula is that it is based on a half-truth: the sequence from new consumption tastes to modernism may describe many cases, but in many other instances the person is arrested at one stage or another on his way to modernism, or even reverts to older patterns. Most of the Types II and III families described in this study are in these categories of arrest and reversion. The explanation suggested by this study is that despite movement away from the traditional pole, tradition still exerts a gravitational pull through kin and friend. This idea is one that could be tested. If it holds some truth, then to bring about modernization the individual must be transplanted wholly from the traditional soil of his family and former reference figures. However, only knowledge in depth of families moving along the scale of types and the path of modernism will help one to begin to unravel these complexities.

3. Another important question concerns the general applicability of the present approach to the study of community change. Are the development of typologies and the delineation of coexistent traditional and contemporary subcultures of any value beyond this local set of neighborhoods? Can such techniques shed light on problems in other parts of Appalachia, parts of rural America, all social systems undergoing social and cultural change, or none of these? Again, a series of comparative studies is needed to answer such questions. More immediate steps must be taken before these larger unanswered questions can be tackled, however.

4. One of the first needs lies in tightening the family typology through more standardized data-gathering techniques. Standard interviews were regarded as ineffective and unreliable at the time this study was carried out. I believe that rapport has been established well enough with many families so that more standardized, survey-type methods could be used in the near future. If interviews of a highly structured nature still do not appear feasible, it is still possible to set up information charts for a number of families, so that data could be collected systematically and stored in a way that one could be certain at a glance whether comparable information were complete for all families or individuals. What is needed is a tighter set of categories for future data-collection of this type. However the mechanics of the process are finally worked out, the family typology, which is in its present form essentially

a set of hypothetical clusterings of family attributes, requires further confirmation.

5. A second step involves devising of a system for describing and a method for accumulating data on the field of forces set by individuals' significant others, so that the reference bind, or cross-pressures, can be more precisely described and compared from one person to another and from one family to another. This task would be facilitated (as would that of strengthening the family typology) if it were found possible to scale traditional and modern values and attitudes held by individuals. The use of such a scale, if it proved feasible, reliable, and valid, would allow the researcher to trace the trajectory (including "conversion" to modernism) of individuals and families over time through the matrix of subcultures in Shiloh.[1]

6. The third—one of the most important immediate tasks that should follow this study—is the assessment of dissatisfactions and pathologies in the community and their distribution throughout various categories of the population; it is in terms of the accomplishment of this task that the present effort is partially justified. There are great methodological problems involved in gauging the extent of these phenomena in populations, subpopulations, and, indeed, individuals, but there are some guidelines and promising horizons in the area. The Health Opinion Survey, which is being validated in a number of widely different settings, is one approach to measuring the experience of personal pathology.[2]

[1] Since this manuscript was completed, promising leads in the measurement of modernism have been reported by Smith and Inkeles, Kahl, and myself. See David H. Smith and Alex Inkeles, "The O-M Scale: A Measure of Individual Modernity," *Sociometry,* XXIX (Dec. 1966), 353-77; Joseph Kahl, *The Measurement of Modernism: A Study of Values in Brazil and Mexico* (Austin: University of Texas Press, 1968); John B. Stephenson, "Is Everyone Going Modern: A Critique and a Suggestion for Measuring Modernism," *American Journal of Sociology,* LXXIV (Nov. 1968).

[2] Dorothea Leighton and others, *The Character of Danger* (New York: Basic Books, 1963), Chap. 7 and Appendix E.

Another source of information on illness lies in the medical records maintained by local doctors, clinics, and hospitals (if permission could be obtained for their use). With regard to the use of these data, however, there is the problem of differential availability of medical services and varying attitudes toward usage among segments of the population. Whatever data are used as indicators of illness, it is imperative that health professionals, perhaps from the field of social psychiatry or community medicine, be represented on the research team for purposes of evaluation of such indexes. Further studies are now in the planning stage.

Appendix B
Notes on Data Collection

Readers of research reports, whether social scientists or laymen, are (or should be) curious about the ways in which the information which makes up "the findings" was obtained. One purpose of these methodological notes is to help satisfy such curiosity and to allow readers a further basis on which to evaluate the "credibility" of the work. The second justification for such an appendix is that it may help future researchers in similar communities to know in simple, human terms, "This is what I did, and these are the problems I encountered." Thus I help repay my debt to former investigators who did the same for me.

In brief, the data were obtained primarily through participant observation. Operationally, this method consisted of semistructured and unstructured interviews plus observation of behavior and interaction of families and family members in their homes, at places of work, in churches, in stores, at bootleggers', in the woods, on riverbanks, and beside the road. Wherever people carry out their lives is where the researcher should be.

Interviews were also conducted with ministers who served churches in the area, health professionals, a welfare caseworker, and other key informants who knew the community but were not directly a part of it. Other secondary information was obtained through official documents and statistics maintained by the county and the state, as well as U.S. Census data. The works by Kaplan, Reina, and Simpson were also helpful. I also drew on my knowledge of the area from three years residence in a nearby mountain county for insights and guidelines for entry into the community. (In spite of warnings to the contrary, rapport was established without difficulty, with the exception of about two weeks when one group in the community suspected me of being an FBI agent.) Books and articles on various aspects of the Southern Appalachian Region or areas within it were used where pertinent. Lastly, data from a state antipoverty "Socioeconomic Survey" conducted in the study county in 1965 were used where they were considered applicable.

At the end of the data-collection period 293 pages of typed, single-spaced field notes had accumulated. Approximately halfway through the summer it became obvious that there would have to be some more systematic way of classifying information as it came in, as the task of organizing the material later would be superhuman. A set of categories was therefore devised in terms of which each paragraph of the field notes could be singly or multiply tagged. The classification was based on theoretical and substantive conceptions of the research problem as formulated in the research proposal and was further elaborated in response to the incoming data itself. Cards were kept for each major category, with entry number, page and paragraph number, so that reference could be made to the field notes for documentation or illustration of a particular topic. This reference system, and the data on which it is based, form the backbone of the research material.

As mentioned elsewhere, the study area as defined for purposes of the research included about 250 households; the entire township contained 347 households in 1960, according to the U.S. Census. During the four months (June–September 1965), I became acquainted with around one-half to three-quarters of the persons living in the study area; although interviews and observations were conducted with a smaller proportion—approximately one-fourth to one-third. These are felt to be conservative estimates. A smaller number of key informants located at different levels and in different areas of the community were relied on heavily.

An effort was made to obtain information on the widest possible variety of families. A conscious effort was also made to oversample the "lower classes," where I felt the least knowledge could be assumed regarding adaptive problems and modes of response. Entries in a log of field notes were made almost daily (exceptions were those days I was not in the field), with conversations recorded verbatim where possible. I took meals with families, visited homes, attended various church services, loafed in stores, accompanied men fishing and hunting, visited places of work, and lent assistance in such chores as hanging tobacco and babysitting, in order to get a closeup view of life on various levels of the community.

One of the major justifications for this kind of approach was the suspected nonfeasibility of such alternatives as standardized interviews or questionnaires. Based on several personal experiences, a "dry run" interview conducted in the spring of 1965, and the reports of my predecessor in the field, I decided to ease into the field setting, allow for a period of gradual researcher-role definition, and concentrate on the establishment of solid rapport. Once firm social relationships were established, I could be more direct in my questioning; use of a technique such as the standard interview schedule, however, would not have been feasible for another year or so. Key informants later agreed that the latter approach would not have worked.

A question frequently asked of community researchers is, "Why did you pick this community?" Although the answer usually implies that only rational, scientific motives influence the choice, both circumstances and personal factors often play a large role. In this case, the study required a changing Appalachian community small enough for one man to comprehend in a relatively brief time. The fact that I knew this state better than others further narrowed the field of choice. Also, of the fifteen or so mountain counties in the state, I was intimately acquainted with only three or four.

Following a tour through these counties, a list of potential study communities was compiled. Three recommended themselves because of their particular advantages. Two were good prospects for study because rapport appeared guaranteed through the kinship of several residents to my wife. The third was an attractive prospect because it had been studied previously, establishing something of a baseline and making easier the entry of a researcher into ground already broken and prepared. At least some people in this third community would know what a social researcher was.

The first two communities were disqualified for the same reason that they had at first seemed attractive. Rapport would have been easy to establish, but only because my role was predefined: I was my wife's husband and her father's son-in-law. As much as one might enjoy these roles personally, they are relatively inflexible roles for the field researcher to adopt. One is expected to attend a certain church, hobnob only with certain families, remain sober—nay, abstinent—and so on. My kinship would have provided a bridge to these people, but a narrow one.

Thus, the third community, Shiloh, was chosen for study. There was only one potential disadvantage in that my predecessors had been there before me, and that, again, raised the possibility that my role as researcher would be predefined in a way that would limit my operation. This problem never became serious.

It is interesting to reflect back on the phases through which the fieldwork passed in the course of the summer and early fall. In retrospect, three stages emerge clearly. The first, which lasted only a week or so, was one of utter floundering and confusion about how to establish myself. This time was spent in setting up my residence in the community in my single room (*sans* family), and in driving through the area repeatedly, noting names on mailboxes and devising homemade maps with every visible household located on them. This knowledge of names and locations proved to be extremely useful as I began to enter conversations with individuals later.

The second stage, which lasted about a month, was one in which the people of the community and I gradually worked out some kind of acceptable definition of who I was and what I was doing. The primary points of entry were the community's several country stores, where I spent hours "loafering" and introducing myself and my work to the storeowners and to the other loafers.

Entry was facilitated by the fact that a few individuals knew or knew of my wife's relatives, even though they were many miles distant. But even kinship identity did not guarantee acceptance, as indicated by the unwillingness of most people to use my name. People needed to know much more about me: Was I someone to "confi*dent*," or trust, was I a "good old boy," was I going to try to "lord it over" anybody because I was an outsider and an educated one at that, was I going to misuse my information?

An event occurred then which started the relationship into the third phase, more rapidly than would otherwise have happened. As I drove out a river road to see an informant one afternoon, I pulled over to allow an oncoming car to pass. The shoulder of the road was more imaginary than real, and the car slid off and turned over the steep riverbank. The car was a total loss, but I was unharmed except for a case of poison ivy.

News of this accident made the rounds of the community like lightning, and my name and reputation were established. People began coming to me with stories of similar events. They wanted me to retell what had happened. Best of all, more people began to call me by name.

The third phase of the field experience was one in which the relationship between researcher and community was broadened and solidified. The data-gathering became more specific and systematic about this time, both because my role was fairly firmly established and because the classification of data-categories was devised during the second month.

One problem encountered was that there were a small number of families who never trusted or accepted me because they were convinced I was a "spy for the FBI." Lingering doubts such as these indicate some lack of success in selling my role properly to the community.

Another problem was the nagging uncertainty about whether I was playing one side or the other of the participant observer role too heavily. Was I sometimes too much a part of the family to see things objectively? Had I allowed myself to become defined as "friend" to the extent that I could no longer ask certain questions? On the other hand, was I asking questions in areas that would bring to ruin the friendship it had taken so long to secure? Was I, perhaps, violating the obligations of friendship by systematically recording conversations and events for use in another context? As Hortense Powdermaker puts it, the field researcher plays the role of both stranger and friend, and the two must be delicately balanced.

A third potential problem is the possible bias that might have grown out of oversampling families at lower levels of living in the community. This oversampling was done intentionally to guard against the natural inclination of the middle-class investigator to acquaint himself with persons most like himself, persons who "speak the same language," and in whose presence he is not so strained. But as a consequence, the picture of families of Type I may suffer from underrepresentation.

The fourth problem also concerns a potential source of bias: the bias of the seasons. Is a family or a community the same in winter as in summer? Would the data have looked markedly different had the research been carried out from November to February? I do not know, and this lack of knowledge is a shortcoming of the study. I was present to observe the shift from summer to fall, when fishing gear is stored and guns are oiled, when children return to school and some mothers return to work, and when another blanket is thrown on the bed at night. The kinds of general cultural patterns described in the text did not change in these two seasons. Still, it should be kept in mind that this is a summer picture, and that the highlights and shadows and accents may have been different in winter or spring.

On the positive side, it appears in retrospect that the researcher-community relationship was a good one all in all, and that the data obtained were of a more reliable and valid nature than had been hoped for. My impression is that if the picture drawn in this study does not reflect the realities of life in Shiloh, it is mainly due to my faulty interpretation and not primarily to faulty data. To an extent unknowable, however, the distinction between data and interpretation is a false one. It may be that other observers with the same degree of objectivity and the same solid rapport would have painted a different but equally valid picture of life in Shiloh. The subjective processes of interpretation guide the search for objective information as well as the final assembling of it.

Index